Following the Drum

Following the Drum
A U. S. infantry officer's wife on the
Texas frontier in the early 1850's

Teresa Griffin Vielé

Following the Drum
*A U. S. infantry officer's wife on the
Texas frontier in the early 1850's*
by Teresa Griffin Vielé

First published under the title
Following the Drum

Leonaur is an imprint
of Oakpast Ltd

Copyright in this form © 2009 Oakpast Ltd

ISBN: 978-1-84677-952-7 (hardcover)
ISBN: 978-1-84677-951-0 (softcover)

http://www.leonaur.com

Publisher's Notes

In the interests of authenticity, the spellings, grammar and place names used have been retained from the original editions.

The opinions of the authors represent a view of events in which she was a participant related from her own perspective, as such the text is relevant as an historical document.

The views expressed in this book are not necessarily those of the publisher.

Contents

Enlisting	9
Recruiting	16
Burlington	20
"Orders"	25
The Tropics	29
Havana	33
New Orleans	40
First Glimpse of Texas	44
Galveston, Texas	48
Brazos St. Jago	54
Fort Brown	59
The Rio Bravo del Norte	67
Ringgold Barracks	72
Davis's Ranch	79
Frontier Piety, Etc.	89
"The Army"	95
Camargo	98
Filibustering	106
Los Indios	117
Camp Life	122
Texas—Past, Present, and Future	129
The Last Tap of the Drum	133

Oh, the drum—it rattles so loud!
There's no such stirring sound
Is heard the wide world round,
As the drum—
      Rückert

To
Winfield Scott,
The Honoured Chief of the Army,
These Pages are Inscribed,

Chapter 1

Enlisting

*There's not a trade a going
Worth knowing! or showing!
Like that from glory growing!*

No recruit ever entered the service with more enthusiasm than I did, or felt more eager to prove himself a soldier.

Military glory, in all its varied phases, had charmed and dazzled me from childhood. My *beau-ideal* hero would have completely lost his identity without his sword and epaulets, and as for my *beau-ideal* heroine, the Maid of Saragossa was a poor, tame, spiritless creature compared to her.

Mars would have gloried in the wonderful female that my imagination loved to paint, and to follow her heroic footsteps seemed a high ambition.

She was a kind of tough, weather-proof, India-rubber woman,

*Six feet high—
Grand, epic, homicidal,*

who could travel over hundreds of miles of prairie on horseback, or follow the train for months on top of a baggage-wagon.

Familiar intercourse with the most savage tribes of Indians was nothing to her! Human sympathy, food, or rest, were mere frivolous weaknesses, necessities of our fallen nature, which she banished from her high-strung mind. A strong energy of character sustained her through the direst emergencies, nothing could unstring her dauntless nerves.

The allurements of dress, petty artifices, tears, or any other little feminine failings she scorned contemptuously! The many minor ills of life she smiled at sardonically.

"The regiment" adored her, and her children (if she had any) were embryo soldiers, arrayed in military baby clothes, cradled in a disabled drum, tucked in with a piece of "star-spangled banner," and teething on a drumstick.

I saw her the witness of many a thrilling and gory scene, with the din of battle in her ear, and stern endurance on her brow. With this vision before my eyes, I enlisted "to follow the drum!"

How many bright dreams of adventure, how much that was delightful and romantic in anticipation now opened before me; all that was fascinating in peril in the wild life of the frontier, rose before my mind in strong and vivid colouring.

The "worldly goods" with which I was endowed in Grace Church, the day of my enlistment, consisted of a mortgage on a camp-kettle, mess chest, bundle of canvas, and set of tent poles, which awaited me at a distant frontier station. Even these few luxuries seemed superfluous to so ardent a campaigner. How was I to live for my country, if I thought too much of personal comfort? the idea was too trifling and effeminate to be considered for an instant; like the French princess, I felt equal to living on cake, in a dearth of bread and butter!

It is true my early training had not been a peculiarly Spartan preparation for endurance and hardship; on the contrary, it would probably have been regarded with stern disapproval by those strict disciplinarians, yet this was more reason for feeling sanguine.

What is more impracticable than the anticipations of youth? Invariably exaggerated—invariably disappointed.

Those faded leaves rustling mournfully through the bleak autumn forests, are the same which, in early spring-time, put forth a delicate *verdure*, to gladden the summer with their beauty.

So experience dimmed the roseate hue of my early day dreams, yet they have been sufficiently realized to tempt a record of them.

The usual course adopted with recruits is, when a sufficient number arc collected, to stow them away in the recesses of a dark old ship, and start them off, to be distributed among the different regiments in the field But having selected a particular arm of the service I was at liberty to join at leisure, in fact, allowed a short reprieve before going upon active duty, and improved the opportunity to revisit that mammoth trap, otherwise called West Point, where the *couleur de rose* of army-life serves as a bait for the unsophisticated, where reality wears the gloss of romance, and military glory appears in its brightest holiday dress, accompanied by all the poetry of war.

Most delusive spot, where even the atmosphere seems heavily freighted with martial music and martial association.

This was not the place to chill a military ardour, but rather to foster it to the utmost.

Our young country, generally so barren of historical association, here presents a strong contrast to that deficiency. Shades of departed heroes haunt each wooded mountain, and reminiscences of

> *Those great spirits, that went down like suns,*
> *And left upon the mountain-tops of death,*
> *A light that made them lovely,*

hallow this nursery of Bellona.

Sculptured monuments, ruined fortress, and crumbling battlement, traces of a glorious past, serve as beacons to guide the stripling soldier to a glorious future.

Like a pilgrim at the shrine of Mecca, in after years I revisit this spot, associated with a youthful admiration of a military life, and not even the dark background of stern reality, that I had seen, could dim its loveliness. West Point, beautiful West Point, how bright are the memories of those who associate their *Love's Young Dream* with thee!

I would gladly have transferred my newly acquired canvas and camp-kettles from Texas to this place, and pitched a tent here for life, had fate and the commander-in-chief so ordained; but it was otherwise arranged by these mighty powers, probably for the reason that the best soldiers were needed on the frontier, the post of danger being the post of honour, as the flower of chivalry is proverbially placed in the van-guard!

The reprieve was longer than had been anticipated, and an indolent summer passed, before orders for duty were received, lingering over the wild woodland beauties of Trenton Falls, and at that glorious indescribable Niagara, with a sail across Lake Erie to Detroit, then the home of General Brady (that aged warrior and veteran of eighteen hundred and twelve). Although past the allotted age of three score years and ten, he drove himself some miles to see, what he was pleased most poetically to term me, "a young pilgrim bound for the land of the Camanches." His fatherly benedictions were quite overpowering.

Awaiting our return from Detroit, at Niagara, was a voluminous package from Washington, having an alarmingly official appearance. It proved to be the first orders for military duty. They were decidedly different from what had been expected; instead of summons to "the tented field," they were instructions to proceed without loss of time to Burlington, Vermont, and there to establish a recruiting rendezvous to enlist soldiers for Uncle Sam. Rather common-place business compared to what had been anticipated.

I knew Vermont by name, and that it was painted green on the atlas at school; there was a time when its cities, rivers, and mountains had been learned by rote, and repeated with the singular velocity peculiar to extreme youth, in happy unconsciousness of their real location, or anything definite in relation to them. Later in life I had heard casual mention made of "Vermont horses," and "Green Mountain boys," but here all knowledge on the subject came to a dead standstill, and I felt quite eager for the hour to arrive, that would give me a clearer insight into this *terra incognita*.

We left Niagara immediately, took a steamer at Queenston for Montreal, and after a delightful sail of twenty-four hours across Lake Ontario (which, in its vast expanse of waters, seems more like the ocean than an inland sea), we entered the waters of the St. Lawrence.

The sail down its rapids is disagreeably exciting; the boat seems threatened every moment to be dashed to pieces, as the pilot skilfully guides it through these perilous mazes. The river rushes impatiently, fretting over the bed of rocks which impedes its course, until it reaches its thousand isles, where it seems to pause, to flow lovingly around their beautiful banks.

They are *very* beautiful; some spreading out for miles in emerald meadow lands, and some only large enough to form the bed of a single forest tree, their banks edged with long grasses, intermingled with wild flowers, drooping over and reflecting graceful fringes in the translucent waters below.

At this point the river seems almost loath to pass on, and does so lingeringly, until it gradually widens into a broad, clear, majestic flow, wider and wider, until it merges itself into that ocean, which at its outset it seemed so eagerly impatient to reach.

Towards evening of the third day after leaving Niagara, we arrived at Montreal, where we stopped for a few days to rest. The un-American air of this place is very striking. In some parts the streets are very narrow, which, combined with the steep roofs of the houses, gives it the air of an old French provincial town. The mixture of French and English inhabitants, commingling in their domestic habits the customs of their native lands, makes a strange *pot-pourri* of manners.

However, the peculiar characteristics of each seem uninfluenced by the other. It would seem as impossible for these two nations to amalgamate, as for oil and water to unite. The happy faculty of adapting one's prejudices to circumstances seems a peculiarly American trait, and may almost be regarded as the national characteristic; the result probably of the gathering together of so many nationalities under the outspread wings of that responsible fowl, the Apis of this people.

One morning we went to the convent of *"Les Sœurs Grises,"* and were shown all over the venerable pile by quite a pretty sister. In an exquisite little Gothic chapel they were celebrating mass for the soul of a priest who had recently died. "We paused at the door, and silently listened to the swell of rich harmony that came rolling in deep volumes from the organ, and filled the air with its full solemn cadence. St. Cecilia herself might have been touching the keys, so inspired the strains that were poured forth, first in the low, sad, prayerful pleadings of fallen humanity, and then in the loud triumphant swell of *the angels around the throne.*

Before we left, I asked our guide why she had become a nun. With downcast eyes, and a sanctified smile, she replied, that "like Mary, she had chosen the better part!" The "better part" is not always the pleasantest, I thought, if wearing a scanty grey gown, and being shut up for life within four stone walls, praying for the forgiveness of sins you never have a chance to commit, constitutes it; and with these rather carnal reflections I passed out of the massive gates, fancying the heavy air that we left behind must have derived some of its oppressive influence from the many sighs for liberty that had for years been borne on it.

We left Montreal the next morning: in the cars for Lake Champlain. Not those miserably contrived cars filled with an indiscriminate crowd of males and females, arrayed in that brown linen uniform, the national costume of the travelling American people, where high and low sit side by side; where the dirty woman with a disagreeably large band-box, and the man who regales himself all too profusely on "plug," seem to vie which shall most contribute to your annoyance; but the private European *coupée,* in which, at some slight difference of expense, a person can travel as if in his own carriage. I have often been surprised, when suffering from travelling annoyances, that in the advancement of luxury these cars have never been introduced upon our railroads.

Stopping at St. John's (the port of entry of Lower Canada), a military station at that time unoccupied (its spreading, empty barracks looking very desolate, with no sounds of life to break the stillness around), we changed cars, and in a short time reached the wharf, and went on board the steamer that was to take us down Lake Champlain, to the point of our destination.

This lake is celebrated even in our land so rich in the picturesque and grand, for the bold and beautiful scenery of its banks. The gigantic mountains seem piled in vast rocky masses, stretching from the water's edge into the clouds, almost beyond sight, their shadows reflected in the lake, as in an azure-tinted mirror. The sloping mountain sides, with deep, wild dells and waterfalls, and piles of fir-clad rocks; the peaceful grain-decked valleys, with rivulets, and towns, and villages discernible among them, formed an ever changing picture of rural beauty.

Towards afternoon we came in sight of Burlington, situated on the banks of the lake, and nestling in the arms of lofty mountain ranges, still clothed in their primeval forests; where the deer and wild animals yet hold possession, and are only intruded upon by the occasional adventurous huntsman.

The bank on which the town lies, is high above the level of the water; the lake, like a silver sheet glittering at its feet, spreads far away, till lost in the base of the mountains that surround it, and whose hundred streams feed its wealth of waters.

Chapter 2

Recruiting

To one whose life has been passed in the bustling, noisy din of a large city, where everybody that you meet in the crowded streets seems eagerly bent on the pursuit of some object that must be attained, if possible, before nightfall; where either hope, or disappointment, or harassing care is stamped on almost every face; there is a novel charm in a sudden change to rural life; a delicious serenity in the atmosphere of a country village, a repose in the calm movements of its inhabitants; the shaded, unpaved streets (cool in the heat of midsummer); the neat green courtyards, and nicely-trimmed flower-beds (from which the smell of pinks, and daisies, and cottage roses seems to breathe out "sweet simplicity"), that is almost incredible.

Few signs of life or animation are to be seen in those quiet cottage homes. Occasionally, perhaps, at the back door of the vine-shaded *piazza*, a placid old lady, seated in her low rocking-chair shelling peas, stopped for a moment by the sight of a humming-bird too daring in its demonstrations to the roses, or a stray fowl in the flower-beds. These will be the events of the day to her, in her quiet, uneventful existence. We smile at its quaint simplicity, but perhaps a sigh of regret is mingled for a moment with our smile.

I supposed that Burlington was one of those simple, unexciting little places, as in time it proved to be, but the first impressions were anything but calm or soothing, as early on the following morning I looked from the windows of the "True

American," through a greenish pane of glass, and through a still more refracting misty rain. Under these depressing influences I saw what appeared to be the most miserable of "one horse towns."

A square inclosed by a whitewashed wooden railing, rendered a disagreeable grey by the rain, ornamented with a pole in the centre, surmounted by one of the numerous and widely-diffused coiffures of the goddess of liberty, and surrounded by the principal stores of the place—this formed the view outside, occasionally animated by one of the damp, moist population, picking their way over the grass-grown brick pavements.

The inside of the hotel was a degree more insufferable, and by way of rendering my gloom more pitiable, the well-meaning landlady provided several "Lady's Books" for my amusement, the contents of which, however, were such a reflection upon even the limited capacities of "ladies" that they gave only fresh cause for aggravation. A gentleman travelling for pleasure, who arrived there the second day after we did, was taken ill and died in the room next to mine, which incident, although perhaps tending to produce a salutary mental influence, was in no way cheering to depressed spirits.

After a fair test of a week, spent in reflections of the most gloomy nature on the ills of life in general, and those of a life in Burlington in particular, it was decided that life at the "True American" was unendurable, and by good luck a cottage was secured on the outskirts of the town. It was everything that could be desired; the velvet lawn in front was green and closely shaven, rose vines clung gracefully around the porch, and not even a cynic could have imagined love contemplating a leap from the latticed window, or another grim visitor with his hand on the old-fashioned knocker. In the rear was a well inclosed with trellis-work, whose moss-covered buckets looked cool and tempting, suggesting, however, to a practical mind that new ones must be immediately obtained, in spite of the romantic charm thrown by the poet around

The moss-covered bucket that hung in the well.

The only drawback to taking immediate possession of this attractive spot was the fact of its being quite devoid of furniture; but we were told that this deficiency could be speedily remedied, by a cleverish sort of fellow named Noble Lovely (which was literally his cognomen). He was immediately applied to, and after an incredible space of time spent in asking questions, he cast his eyes around upon his household gods, and said: "Well, neow, what would you think of a second-hand red plush sofy, and a yellow chanie spittoon to begin with?"

This proposal was beyond human endurance, and as these articles were not considered absolutely indispensable in an unpretending *ménage*, it was deemed advisable to withdraw, which induced Mr. Lovely to speedily make the necessary arrangements; and, to use the technical Yankee expression, "the bargain was closed," to the inexpressible delight of the shrewd and (not over) Noble Lovely, who "realized quite a little considerable" in consequence. From the first I imbibed a strong dislike to this class. I do not think these feelings were entirely without foundation.

In fact I may candidly confess, that I never could feel the necessary degree of enthusiasm in reference to our New England brethren, or their fundamental principles of the innate depravity of the Pope, intense sympathy tor that coloured "army of martyrs" south of Mason and Dixon's line, or the infallibility of the pilgrim fathers. On the contrary, I conceive the Pope may be an excellent good man, that those suffering and bleeding bondsmen may have an occasional ray of sunshine on their dreary path of life, and that the way in which the heroes of Plymouth Rock burned Quakers and eccentric old ladies was, to say the least, unamiable.

We all, however, have our prejudices, in common with them, and I suppose, would hardly be human without them.

Six months, comprising the severest of the year, were passed in Burlington in ardent endeavours to add to the United States forces as many deserters from the ranks of her majesty of England, as could persuade the recruiting sergeant they were regularly discharged, and the doctor that they were "able bodied."

They were a reckless set of men, generally under five-and-twenty years of age, a collection probably of black sheep from as many different families; some of them well educated, and undoubtedly of highly respectable parentage. I can give them the highest diploma for gallantry.

In fact there seems to be something in a uniform that calls forth this quality in its wearer in the highest degree. Apply a uniform to a man, and like a mustard plaster, it seems to draw all that is inflammable to the surface.

One or another of the recruits was always at hand, and in turn they scoured the country to get anything that it was not easy to obtain in the town. I often pitied them as they flaunted about in their gay trappings (like sheep dressed for the slaughter), to think how soon their existence would probably terminate, on some march across the prairies, in the sickly swamps of Florida, or on the perilous Indian scout, shot by the poisoned arrow of a Camanche or Sioux. Between them and the *gamins* of Burlington, there existed a continual feud.

One of the recruits (whose bump of combativeness was so wonderfully developed that it kept continually knocking his cap off his head, unless he resorted to a strap) had to be sent off, so constantly were his pugnacious tendencies exhibited in heading what he graphically termed "little heat ups" or "knock clowns," between the contending parties. The soldiers were called U. S. males (mails) by their opponents, who even went so far as to make distant allusions to the serjeant's wife as a U. S. female.

This remark was followed by an exciting row, which terminated in a series of mutilations and dark rims around the visual organs of most of the gallant recruits, a squad of whom were forthwith despatched to Fort Columbus—among them, that troublesome but "bold soldier boy" with the annoying cap, who, it was discovered, hailed from Kilkenny, which most satisfactorily accounted for the excrescences behind his ears.

Chapter 3

Burlington

Startling incidents never occurred in Burlington. None ever bad occurred there, and none probably ever will. The advent of a stranger was an important event, so few people ever came there. A stray artist, or lingering traveller, fascinated by the shadows of the Adirondack, as they fell into the lake, or an occasional acquaintance passing through on the way from the White Mountains to Saratoga, were always welcome visitors.

The most unfailing resource was driving and riding. The beautiful scenery, the bracing October air, and the forest-clad mountains, arrayed in their autumnal robes of crimson, amethyst, and royal purple, rendered out-of-door exercise peculiarly exhilarating and attractive.

The term "Vermont horses" was soon after our arrival most potently realized in the possession of a pair of dapple greys worthy of the horse-flesh reputation of their native State, with arching necks, long silken manes and tails, eyes full of spirit, and feet that seemed to disdain the ground. To drive them was emphatically "driving a team!" They went miles and miles every day, like the wind, either in harness or under the saddle, and were the "Green Mountain boys" that left the deepest impression on my heart. Country pleasures are enchanting, if we can forget the more alluring ones of a civilized metropolis!

One of the most attractive drives in the neighborhood is over a fine, well-beaten road to Rock Point, the picturesque residence of Bishop Hopkins, of the Episcopal church of this State.

His place is beautifully situated north of the town, on a small promontory that stretches into the lake. It is a farm of some extent; the drive from the gate to the house, of about a quarter of a mile, through a park and lawn (that owe much to Nature and little to Art for their woodland beauties), is quite imposing. Fine forest trees, scattered in groups, abound all over the domain. The house is quite unpretending, but its situation is magnificent, commanding a view of the lake, and the town of Burlington in the distance, with a gorgeous background of mountain scenery, made up of the numerous bright lights and deep shadows peculiar to this region of country.

The interior of the house bears impress of the home of the scholar and man of taste; the library opening on a *piazza* by an enormous oriel window, from which, through clambering honeysuckle vines, you can enjoy one of the grandest pictures ever sketched by nature on earth's fair tablet.

The walls of the library are covered with paintings, the work of the artistic hand of Bishop H., who is generally to be found sitting in this room at his desk, writing tracts and religious essays for the press, to send forth into the world from his secluded home, like the sower of holy writ casting forth his seed.

His tall athletic form, grey hair, somewhat stern expression of countenance and rigid views of life, reminded me of the apostles of old, or our Huguenot fathers, who so readily sacrificed their worldly interests "for conscience sake."

The autumn soon deepened into the gloom of November, the weather became cold and bleak. The ground was strewn with fallen leaves. The

> *Wind, that grand old harper, smote*
> *His thunder harp of pines.*

Soon the earth arrayed itself in a holiday attire of six feet of dazzling snow, the trees brilliant with icicles shone radiantly in the sunlight, and the hardy little snow birds, scattered over this brilliant carpet of the north, were the only vestige of the summer that had fled into the past—while the gay inspiriting sound of sleigh-bells seemed to give warning that the season for Christmas festivities was approaching.

The morning after the first snow-storm we awoke in utter darkness, and found ourselves completely embedded in snow, which reached to the top of the second story windows; but by noon eight or ten of the gallant recruits had cut a passage to the house, and removed the greater part of the snow-drift in which we had been buried alive.

The sleighing was unsurpassable, but the intense cold of the frosty cutting air spoiled the enjoyment of it. At times exposure was next to impossible; the thermometer fifteen degrees below zero was no uncommon thing. Anyone who has passed a winter in the northern part of Vermont on the side of one of its bleak mountains, and on the shores of its great lake, would not be surprised that Sir John Franklin has never been discovered, but that any human being has ever returned alive from the arctic regions of "Jack Frost."

Christmas was heralded by sleigh-loads of evergreens driven towards the church, and even candies and penny toys made their appearance in the shop-windows to tempt this prudent race from their wonted frugality.

The arrival of several American officers, detained here by a storm on their way to a court-martial, and the presence of several young Canadian guardsmen bound to New York for a "spree," tempted me to essay a Christmas-Eve ball.

The house was decorated with evergreens, and on truly republican principle there was not a pretty girl in Burlington who was not asked.

On the appointed evening at about seven o'clock (sweet simplicity!) the guests commenced to arrive.

Two fiddlers and a drummer-boy, with a cold in his head, formed the band; the ball terminated at midnight, proving a great success.

It was however quite late in the small hours, before our officers and the "royal Canadian guardsmen" had drunk their last libation to the Queen, and "Jimmy Polk of Tennessee." They finally parted, with many promises of soon meeting again; but in the army, such promises amounted to an absurdity, for beyond

Wafts of song
From arm-linked youths as they meandered home!

and several cards containing five or six aristocratic names apiece, we have never heard from them since.

A few months saw us on the confines of Mexico, while they were journeying towards the burning plains of India.

One individual who figured on this occasion is worth a word of notice. A person representing himself as an English gentleman, travelling in this country for amusement and information, had arrived in Burlington that autumn, and taken rooms at the hotel. Although not a particularly attractive or agreeable man, he was not the opposite, and in dearth of other society, became quite a *habitué* at some of the most respectable citizens' houses. He had a dog-cart, horses, guns, and pointers, and professed to be a great sportsman. He was very devoted in his attentions to a young Canadian girl, and a handsome widow, who were considered by the public to be rivals, between whom this gay deceiver was wavering.

He had had very extensive dealings with the bank, which at first imposed on the community, and then excited suspicion. One day he suddenly disappeared, and no traces of him were to be found, leaving his lady-loves disconsolate, and carrying with him quite a sum of money that he had obtained by fraud.

The following year he was traced to a secluded western village, where a repetition of similar amorous and financial performances had rendered suspicion certainty, and finally lodged him safely in a penitentiary, where he could expiate his rascality by the harmless pastime of hewing stone or making shoes. It is easy to picture him in the mind's eye, in a woven wool roundabout and trousers, one yellow leg and arm, and one black, with a cap to match, pursuing the even tenor of his way on a daily meal of bean broth and ship biscuit, his conversation limited to an occasional whisper through the register tubes to the prisoner in the next cell, at the risk of a severe penalty for even this slender mode of communication with his kind.

I never could define this person's position; no aspirated *h* betrayed the low-born Englishman, and, judging by his conversation, his education must have been quite superior; banking and the fair sex were evidently his weaknesses, and the rocks on which he foundered.

Variety is to life what rum is to an omelette; it gives it piquancy, or to be still more original, it is its spice; and at the time I thought, if I had stayed at home, I never should have come in contact with that peculiar specimen of ornithology yclept a jail bird. After events, however, proved that candidates at least for this position were not so rare, even in a New York drawing-room, as the unsophisticated might suppose.

He who runs may read!

Chapter 4

"Orders"

In January orders arrived from Washington to break up the recruiting rendezvous at Burlington, and join the first regiment of United States Infantry at Ringgold Barracks, Texas, on the Lower Rio Grande.

After the arrival of a dispatch of this nature from the War Department, there is no time allowed to pause and reflect. Prompt obedience is the first lesson a soldier must learn.

Theirs not to make reply,
Theirs not to reason why,
Theirs but to do and die.

So, after twenty-four hours' notice, we quitted Burlington forever, passing down the lake on a dismal winter day, the steamer breaking with difficulty through fields of ice that blocked its passage to Whitehall, where we were detained several hours, waiting for the northern train of cars that was to convey us to Albany. Whitehall lies at the foot of Lake Champlain, in the State of New York. During the short time spent there I saw more specimens of the genus loafer than I had imagined could exist—from the grey-haired, seedy, dock *habitué*, to the stinted, half-starved, little object, who seemed hardly large enough to hold the cigar in his mouth, which he affected to enjoy extremely, although it evidently disagreed with him.

One importunate vendor of illustrated newspapers, about a foot and a half high, with garments so wonderfully ragged, that if once taken off they could never by any possibility have been put on again, tried every inducement he could conceive of to tempt purchasers into the expenditure of sixpence.

One man, to get rid of him, said he did not know how to read. "But you can look at picter*s*" said the indomitable young merchant, and his shrewdness secured a customer!

I knew instinctively that he came from Vermont, and had been taught in one of its district schools to count his pennies as soon as he could talk, and that the chief end and aim of man's existence was to accumulate "York shillings." I thought it quite probable that fifty years hence would see him "a merchant prince." rolling in wealth acquired by this same "business tact!" As has been frequently before remarked, we are a great and wonderful people!

The principal public buildings at Whitehall seemed to be railroad depots and refreshment saloons, a sight of whose edibles was anything but refreshing. Trains of cars leave here for every point of the compass, and in consequence newspaper and lozenge boys "here most do congregate," and successful pickpockets revel in rifled items.

There is here a large, well-built Catholic church, and the money that should have gone legitimately towards patching the elbows and cobbling the shoes of the vagrant inhabitants, had evidently been used to pay penance for their numerous sins.

The cars took us that evening to Albany, that most respectable of Dutch Reformed cities, whose more venerable inhabitants have lost so few of their honest Dutch prejudices against modern innovation; yet who does not regret that their quaintly gabled homesteads are yearly becoming rarer, and their crumbling moss-grown gravestones, and great family bibles with brass clasps (reverently preserved), are all that is left to tell of the Diedrichs and Johannas, and their fair-haired Katalinas, who came there a hundred years ago, from the Netherlands?

On arriving in New York we found a further reprieve, by which we were spared the disagreeable necessity of being accompanied on a transport ship by two or three hundred valiant recruits, who, as the sequel proved, indulged themselves on the voyage by the exciting pastime of a mutiny, which resulted in the shooting of that chivalrous recruit who had caused so much excitement and trouble in Burlington. He recovered, however, from his wounds, and became afterwards an excellent soldier, who has probably ere this

Met a foeman worthier of his steel

than his commanding officer.

The departure for Texas was delayed until the month of April, when we sailed in the steamship *Ohio*, bound for New Orleans, *via* the Havana. Its gallant commander (commanders are always gallant, or ought to be) was so kind to me, that I would add a public eulogy to the many private ones I have pronounced on him, if it were in good taste to do so. His invariable kindness and good-humour were almost a cure for sea-sickness, that most doleful of all the maladies which flesh is heir to.

There was on board a very agreeable and amusing party, and in the informal intercourse of a sea voyage the time passed rapidly.

The only drawback to its pleasure was the slight one of being totally deprived of "balmy sleep," by a nightly row in the opposite state-room, not at all propitious to the cultivation of "nature's sweet restorer!" It was occupied by a family of (two or three dozen, I should think) small infants, under the charge of an old black "aunty," who was kept in a continual state of excitement, all being sea-sick at the same time; and to the daily inquiries of the head of the family after their progress, I heard the invariable and discouraging reply of "sick, massa! all hands!"

We were a good deal in sight of land, and kept in view the shores of Maryland, Delaware, and the Carolinas. When off the coast of Florida we came near enough to land to see the wreckers at work on a large ship, that had been abandoned by its crew.

These wreckers are a miserable, unprincipled, ignorant race, who live on the sea-coast, where, on account of its peculiar formation, accidents arc very numerous. Their only means of subsistence depending upon the losses and misfortunes of their fellow-men, they seem to be the last traces left, in North America, of the buccaneer or sea-robber race.

The same afternoon, some hours later, in passing the reefs, we saw a brig with its flag of distress up. Our captain ordered the small boat to their relief, and they soon landed on our deck fifteen passengers, besides the crew; they were all Spaniards, who had left Cuba but a few days before, with a cargo of sugar, bound for Spain, but were obliged, at this early period of their voyage, to abandon their ship and cargo to the mercy of the wind, the waves, and the wreckers, and were soon landed, by us at the Havana. We were now within the current of the Gulf Stream.

That night of moonlight on a southern sea! It seems a dream in retrospect. The moon mingled its soft light with the balmy delicious air as it arose, and faintly illuminated the still blue waters; while spicy odours from the shore told that it was Cuba that lay before us, stretching in that misty, indistinct line in the distance. Cuba, that beautiful gem of the Mexican golf, whose breath is fragrance, whom Nature seems to have chosen (in one of her most prodigal freaks) to have showered with all the rarest and most precious of her gifts.

Later on that night, bright and luminous above us, rose the Southern Cross, emblazoned in characters of gold upon the deep ground-work of the midnight sky.

CHAPTER 5

The Tropics

Yet waft me from the harbour's mouth,
Wild wind! I seek a warmer sky,
And I will see before I die
The palms and temples of the South.
                    Tennyson

The next morning we awoke in full sight of the island of Cuba, and by ten o'clock a.m. had dropped anchor in the harbour of Havana (said to be the finest in the world).

Who will ever forget their first impression of the tropics! The rich emerald of the luxuriant verdure, the glowing, rosy tint of sky and sea, and the delicious, dreamy softness of the air! The palm trees, in full relief against the warmly-tinted skies, call to mind the loves of Paul and Virginia. Breathing the atmosphere seems like reading a chapter from the Koran while

In every change of earth and sea,
Breathes the deep soul of poesy.

The battlements of Moro Castle, apparently rising abruptly from the sea, the spires and brilliantly-coloured palaces of Havana, glittering in the sunlight of a summer morning, the background of the mountains of Sierra del Cobre, studded with country-seats and picturesque hamlets, formed a picture at once novel and strikingly beautiful.

After the usual preliminaries, and a most ceremonious visit from the Spanish authorities, who came in a brightly-decorated barge with striped red and white awnings, and the Spanish flag in the stern, manned by twenty liveried oarsmen, only surpassed in the gaudy taste of their dress by the officers, whose uniforms, ribbons, and stars seemed much more abundant than the occasion required. They finally assured themselves that we were only a peaceful set of travellers, and not an invading army of filibusters. The passports were duly made out and paid for, and then these worthies departed. It was no great deprivation to lose sight of their ugly, swarthy laces, that beamed with anything but benevolence or beauty.

Finally, we passed down the ladder at the vessel's side to the boat that awaited us, were rowed swiftly to the shore, and landed on a dock, piled with sugar barrels and boxes, on which reclined groups of negro slaves in the lightest possible attire, while others were loading and unloading cargoes.

Many younger scions of Africa were loitering about, who proved, by licking the sides of the molasses barrels, that the propensities of youth are alike in all climes and among all races.

In Havana, garments, like discretion or experience, come with age; they are quite unknown to the younger portion of the inhabitants.

We soon found ourselves in a hotel, quite novel in all its phases to the untravelled American. Saloons paved with tessellated marble, and shaded by blinds to a cool twilight; the windows open to the floor, and latticed with iron trellis-work, looking out on a court-yard luxuriant with tropical verdure; the windows have no sashes or glass to shut out from the interior the lightest breath of summer. The massive front doors of all the houses are ornamented with iron bars, made to stand attacks from without, so continually do the upper classes live in dread of revolution and assault. Divans of cane-work and rocking-chairs seem to be the principal articles of furniture.

We were almost immediately shown to a room, floored with brick, and provided with iron furniture, on the way up obtaining a large bunch of exotics, bought from a young negress flower-girl, who was seated at the head of the stairway.

At dinner, the table was piled with rare flowers and fruits, and the "imprisoned sunshine" of the golden hock, and crimson claret, round the miniature icebergs in the "flowing cup," with the piles of pineapples, bananas, pomegranates, and nectarines, seemed entirely to take from the stern reality of roast beef. In fact, the meals here reminded me of the tea-parties which Milton describes, as given by Eve to her angelic guests in the beautiful bowers of Eden.

After dinner comes "the *siesta*," and then the recreations of the day commence. A dress of muslin, *sans chapeau*, is sufficient protection against the weather, and all that custom exacts for the "*toilette*" of an afternoon drive.

The *volante*, the vehicle of this country, is at the door before six o'clock. To those who have ridden in them, a description would be superfluous, and to those who have not, it will be almost impossible. Its lazy motion as it moves along hardly disturbs the soft atmosphere.

Our *volante*, hired by the day during our short stay, was the property of a Cuban nobleman, who had retired to his country-seat among the mountains, and left it and his coachman in town, to be hired by strangers. He must probably have been "hard up," judging by this proceeding, but this is merely a natural surmise. It was "got up" in most gorgeous style, and in the gaudy taste peculiar to Spanish-Americans. Its body, what we would call a tilbury on a large scale, the top shifting, the pole double the length of one of our ordinary vehicles, which consequently leaves quite a space between the body of the *volante* and the mules that draw it. These latter were fat, and beautifully groomed, and trapped in gold and crimson cloth, one of them being ridden *à la postillion* by the driver.

The Cuban "whips" are in themselves quite a study. A jacket, *à la Grecque*, of crimson cloth, embossed with gold, falling open and exhibiting a gaily trimmed vest, and linen edged with deep lace ruffles, tights, and top boots, inlaid, and finished round the top with gold fringe, and a cord and tassel of the same. A beaver hat, with a broad gold band and cockade, complete their stylish outfit.

These liveries are always gay, sometimes elegant, and at times bordering on the grotesque.

A *volante*, with all its charms, would be as much out of place in a city of the United States, as a trotting wagon and pair of fast horses would be at the Plaza de Armas of Havana.

Our first drive embraced a great deal. It first took us through the town, towards the suburbs; it was the hour of evening vespers, and the chimes were tolling out their call to devotion. The Spanish *donnas*, in their black lace veils, holding rosaries in their hands, followed by negro slaves in livery bearing their prayer-books, looked very picturesque.

In some places the streets are so narrow, that opposite neighbours could shake hands from the windows, if so inclined.

Negresses, selling bouquets and bunches of loose flowers, spread out in tempting array in large flat shallow baskets, which they balance gracefully on their heads when they walk, are to be seen in all directions sitting at the corners of the streets, where they display their beautiful articles of merchandise.

There is, I was told, quite a large free coloured population in Havana. Here you often meet with the genuine native of Southern Africa, caught from the wilderness by the slave trader, but a few years before.

If we could compare these brutal animal features, and lack of all intellect, to the "Uncle Toms" and "Aunt Chloes" of our land, we might be convinced that from one point of view at least, slavery might be regarded as a blessing instead of "a curse."

CHAPTER 6

Havana

A drive to the "Bishop's Garden" through the suburbs of Havana, seemed like shifting scenes from fairy land. Beautiful villas skirted the road on either side, some of a pale blue colour, some rose, and other delicate hues of stucco, surrounded by gardens beyond description lovely—while delicious

Odour was upon the breeze,
Sweet thefts of rose and lemon trees.

We could see directly through the houses (the doors and windows being open and latticed with iron) into the gardens in the rear, where, among fountains and arbours, children with their attendants were scattered in every direction.

On each *piazza* were long rows of Yankee rocking chairs filled with different members of the family, rocking slowly backward and forward, producing a very absurd effect, and giving a good idea of the enervating habits of the inhabitants.

Some of the nobility live in a style of eastern magnificence, with an enormous retinue of slaves in attendance.

When we arrived at the bishop's garden we alighted at the entrance. It was the former residence of the Roman Catholic bishop of Cuba, about five or six miles out of the city. The house had been destroyed by a hurricane some years before, but the ruins still remain. We entered these beautiful domains on foot, leaving our *volante* at the entrance.

How can I find words to describe the overwhelming surfeit

that this garden gives to the sense of the beautiful; every tropical plant and tree grows in unprimed and wild luxuriance. Cape jessamine hedges, japonicas, tea-roses, and passion flowers, in profusion. I remember one of these latter vines, running up the side of a giant mahogany tree, its foliage of deep green, bright with blossoms, waving about its branches like a richly gemmed drapery.

We saw here the remains of a former zoological garden, at present but poorly maintained. Among other novelties was an alligator, but my preconceived ideas of this animal, gathered from the graphic pen of Peter Parley, who paints him and the duplicity of his character in such vivid and fearful terms, made my visit to him of very short duration. His terrible jaws and deceitful expression of countenance, seemed fully to justify all the censures that his various biographers have bestowed upon him.

The birds were very attractive; their bright plumage of various shades of lemon and rose colour, and their graceful forms, were beautiful even to an ignorant person, whose dim recollection of their Latin names and classifications was almost disgraceful in these palmy days of the general diffusion of knowledge.

Several negroes were here at work with balls and chains attached to their ankles, which served the purposes of anchors; they were convicts, who were thus employed by the government, to keep the grounds in order, their sole attire a *jupon* of about a foot long, resembling a scanty ruffle, around the waist.

Magnolia, pomegranate, and pineapple trees, coffee, tobacco, and sugar-cane, were growing in the open air. Everything that we are only, used to see in dried specimens, in stores, or on the table, here grew, as the most hardy grain does in our climate.

Simple existence is enjoyment in this delicious atmosphere, so balmy the air, so exquisite the perfume wafted on each breeze. Yet, like the whitened sepulchre, within all is corruption. A tarantula or scorpion lies in ambush under many a lovely blossom, and the breath of *the pestilence that walketh in the noonday*, is mingled with the perfumed breeze that is wafted over this beautiful "gem of the ocean," this waning "lone-star" that pleads through its silent and crushed people to join our constellation.

To the Cubans the word freedom is a mockery; the suspicious and vigilant watchfulness practised by the Spanish authorities is almost incredible to us.

It must be the impulse of every generous heart, who gains the merest insight into the dreadful system of taxation and oppression, suffered by the inhabitants of this colony of Spain, to become a filibuster in feeling if not in principle.

The people are eagerly listening for the watchword of revolution, and it is the earnest wish of all but the emissaries of the Spanish throne, to see Cuba enrolled in our union.

Philanthropy more than aggrandizement should be our motive for its annexation.

In returning from our drive, as we passed along, "the light from alabaster lamps" in the interior of the houses, mingling with the soft rays of the moon outside, lighted up the gardens and the porches, and gave a subdued effect to the surrounding country. As we approached the town, and entered the Paseo de Isabella, the gas-lights began to glimmer from the city, the marble statues shone pale and ghostly in the moon's light, and the glistening flowers, laden with evening's dews, sent forth an odour, with which the air was heavily laden.

This *paseo*, called after the present queen-mother of Spain, is ornamented by her statue, taken in childhood, the innocent expression of its soft infantile features bearing but little impress of the characteristics which now distinguish that royal lady.

It is a miniature park, laid out in drives and foot-paths, and ornamented with flower-beds, fountains, marble seats, and statuary.

The opera-house (which at this season was closed), a sumptuously furnished cafe, and some of the magnificent palaces of the aristocracy, front this *Paseo*.

After lingering here awhile, we drove to the Plaza des Armas, or Champs de Mars, fronting the residence of the governor, a marble palace surrounded by a garden, in the centre of which was a colossal fountain, surmounted by a statue of one of the numerous Spanish Ferdinands.

On the opposite side of the *plaza* the government buildings and barracks are situated.

Every evening the military band plays in front of the governor's palace for several hours. Spanish soldiers lounge about with their inseparable *cigaritas*, while the officers pay their *devoirs* to the various *donnas*, seated in their *volantes*, who come here to see their acquaintances and listen to the band.

They appeared to me very coarse, with swarthy skins, and inclined to embonpoint. However, by such a mere casual glance, it is hardly fair to judge on so delicate a subject as personal beauty.

The populace, divested of their squalor by the magic of the moon's light, were picturesquely grouped around, while the exquisite flood of Italian music that swelled on the soft air, through the hum of the audience, seemed even more beautiful than such melody invariably is.

The German school of music is certainly very beautiful, and profoundly scientific; and that of France and Switzerland, inspiriting and gay; but the strains of Italy seem to breathe the passion and poetry of its sunny clime, and appeal more directly to the heart and sensibilities.

The ice-cream saloons or cafés of Havana are a favourite place of resort on the summer evenings. The principal one was very attractive; a cool fountain in the centre, throwing up a single jet and falling in a million sparkling drops on a collection of rare flowers and shells, which lay surrounding its base, and glittering with spray, as if set with so many brilliants. The ceiling was open, and far beyond could be seen the skies, faintly illumined by the moon, and gemmed with innumerable stars. Scattered over the tessellated marble floor were marble tables and seats, and marble pillars supported the arched and *frescoed* walls. The ices are very poor, and have only their coolness to recommend them.

All foreigners that visit Havana consider it incumbent on them not to leave there without purchasing a pineapple handkerchief and a Spanish fan (generally manufactured in Paris), and in consequence the hotel is hourly besieged with numerous venders of these articles. Among them I observed more than one Yankee; this, however, is universally the case where trade is pushed with any amount of vigour.

It is said that the day after the city of Mexico was taken, and entered in triumph by General Scott and his victorious army, one of this enterprising race set up a gentlemen's furnishing store, next door to the halls of the Montezumas, and put out placards advertising "gents' patent arm-slings," and "the only genuine gunshot-wound pain exterminator," warranted to cure at shortest notice! There was at the time naturally a great demand for these articles, and if that son of New England did not "realize" something it was owing to no lack of effort on his part.

We visited a cigar manufactory, and saw "the weed" in every variety of form, and in every stage, from the original article, fresh from the fields, to the crisp little *cigaritos*, lying together in tempting bunches, and tied with yellow and crimson ribbons, in boxes labelled "Santa Rosa," "Opera," &c. &c. They were soon to be outward bound from their native land—destined to fill the pauses of life to many a club lounger, to accompany reverie, and impart bliss generally to the happy mortals into whose possession fate might throw them.

The markets of Havana at this season were naturally attractive places; one department for flowers, fruit, and birds, was very interesting and refreshing, attended entirely by negresses.

The object that most attracted my attention, and left the deepest impression on my mind, while in Havana, was the tomb of Christopher Columbus, the discoverer of this island. Nearly four centuries have passed since then. It was within the last of these that his remains were removed from Spain to one of the minor West India islands, but found a final grave in Havana.

This fair young world that revealed itself first to his enraptured vision, seems a more fitting resting-place for its discoverer than ungrateful Spain or the land that gave him birth.

He had always been one of my favourite heroes, and I had

loved to dwell on his almost inspired career—the high-wrought enthusiasm that led him to imagine it his mission to discover a New World—that glowing imagination that was but the pioneer to great deeds. Impelled by fate to the performance of this work, to execute it in spite of the conflicting influences, at first of discouragement, and then of the mutiny of his shrinking and treacherous companions; totally unsympathized with by these terror-stricken men in the vast unknown deserts of ocean; yet, in spite of their threats, urging on his frail bark, and finally landing in safety on the New World's shore—one of the sublimest triumphs ever afforded to man, borne with unparalleled modesty!

There is no combination of character so admirable, to my mind, as that which unites practical common-sense, strong energy, and firmness of purpose with a glowing and enthusiastic imagination.

A mind that can disregard the misrepresentations and discouragements of an unjust unappreciative public, manfully fight its way through adverse circumstances, smiling at the follies of a world that misunderstands it; confident in a conscious truth and honesty of purpose, pursuing a steadfast undeviating course, uninfluenced but by its preconceived ideas of right—

That pure high constancy which flies right on,
As swerveless as a bullet, to its mark;—

coming out eventually at the end of its career, like a glorious sunset at the close of a clouded day, supremely beautiful, eliciting unasked and universal admiration.

The tomb of Columbus is situated on the Plaza des Armas, surrounded by trees. The monument is plain and unpretending, bearing a *basso-relievo* likeness of the great discoverer, with an inscription in Spanish—

To Castile and Leon Columbus gave a new world.

Brief yet ample sentence!

The world was cold,

And he went down like a lone ship at sea.
And now the fame that scorned him while he lived
Waits on him like a menial.

Chapter 7

New Orleans

We left Havana with many regrets. In the few days passed there, enough of its beauties and pleasures had been tasted not to satiate. I left it with all its dreamy and indolent beauty deeply impressed upon my mind—

Flowers and rills live sunnily
In gardens of my memory,

but none in more vivid colouring than those of Cuba. As its palm-trees, that had brought with them so new and delightful a sensation, passed from my sight, I felt that with them a dream had vanished; a bright scene had passed by in the panorama of existence.

Two more days at sea, and we arrived where the dark and murky waters of the Mississippi empty themselves into the blue waves of the Mexican Gulf. At this point the dividing line of the waters was distinctly visible.

The scenery as the boat entered the principal channel of the Mississippi is peculiarly dreary and desolate. The sea-board on either side is covered with miles of low swampy green salt plains, with lagoons, or natural canals, cut in every direction. The river pours itself into the sea, through three passes. I suppose the reason why it is called the "Father of Waters" is, because it has so many little mouths to feed!

We paused at the mouth of the river for a few moments to take in the pilot, whose hut, situated on one of these dreary plains, seemed a concentration of all that was desolate. Nothing can be more dreary, solitary, or devoid of all life, than these wastes of marshy, low, flat lands—no vegetation but salt meadow grass in sight. A strange place to choose out of the whole world for a home, and yet there were children clustering around the door-steps. To its master it probably did not bear the dreary aspect it did to the passing traveller. So differently in life do we form our estimates.

We spent the day on deck watching the negroes on either side of the river at work in the sugar-cane and cotton-fields—the overseer on horseback riding to and fro among them. The negro cabins seemed comfortable, neat, and admirably adapted to the climate and their wants. The tall chimneys of the sugar distilleries rose up against the sky, with clouds of smoke issuing from them. Then the pleasure-grounds, gardens, and house of the planter, the *piazzas* supported by graceful pillars, and ornamented with urns, filled and running over with creeping plants, with terraces of roses and flowers of varied hue, and children on the lawn with their sable nurses, whose saffron-coloured bandannas bloomed brighter than any blossom around.

The morning air was soft and delicious, the waters danced and sparkled in the sunlight, while the shores were bright with verdure and human beings. The negroes singing at their work presented a picture of contented industry that would quite have amazed the Duchess of Sutherland, and other less illustrious but quite as philanthropic ladies, who need not come as far as they do to find food for their surplus sympathies.

Late in the afternoon the Crescent City came in sight, and towards evening we found ourselves landed and established at the St. Louis Hotel, which, since the burning of the St. Charles, has been the famous hotel of the South-West. The planters along the river generally come here on a visit every winter, bringing their wives and daughters to enjoy the gaieties of this great metropolis. Bridal parties are wonderfully numerous.

The men at the St. Louis employ their time in drinking juleps and other beverages in the great rotunda of the hotel, which apartment is a gorgeous affair, most sumptuously fitted up, the centre terminating in a lofty dome, which lights it from above through stained glass windows. Here, over various descriptions of drinks, the principal business of the city is transacted, cotton Bold, sugar bought, fortunes made and lost—enormous gambling transactions, looked upon with leniency by the world, and called business.

While the men are enjoying the delights of this luxurious bar-room, the women employ themselves in dressing elaborately several times a day, and sitting in the gorgeous and extensive drawing-rooms, forming quite a study for a spectator, from the exquisite Parisian quiet of some *piquante* Creole to the flashy, exaggerated finery of a Western village *belle*. As in almost all public assemblies in this newly forming world, ignorance and bad taste predominate.

From hotel life more can be seen of New Orleans society than in other cities. A stranger can form no definite idea from it alone; but judging from an evening's insight at a *soirée* musicale at the British Consul's, I should imagine it was very elegant in its tone.

The Creole women dress beautifully; their mode of *coiffure* is a study, rich glossy masses of hair rolled around their heads in classic and artistic style.

The only drive of any importance in the neighbourhood of New Orleans is the Shell Road, which terminates at Lake Ponchartrain, where the steamers start for Mobile. This drive offers but few attractions; a canal runs on one side, and a ditch on the other. It is a great resort for "fast" men (for which New Orleans is celebrated), who here run their horses at large.

The canal serves the double purpose of draining a neighbouring marsh, and navigation. In fact, the whole surface of the land is, in a great measure, a marsh. At the cemetery, when they dig down two feet for a grave, they come to water. It is found necessary to use iron boxes, and bury the dead above ground, in brick graves like a Dutch oven.

There is a dull unprogressive aspect about everything connected with New Orleans—there seems to be a stagnation in public spirit, The habit of lounging and drinking in bar-rooms prevails to a fearful extent. All the principal public buildings are the work of Government. There seems to be but little private enterprise, which must be from the effect of the enervating climate and the continually fluctuating state of the market, which is at times in a state of wild elation, and, by an overflow of the river, may be reduced, in twenty-four hours, to a state of utter and hopeless depression, closely resembling the varying spirits of the Micawber family as described by Mr. Dickens.

There is little reason to wonder that men, brought up under these peculiar influences, should become enervated, and more prone to lounge at their ease, than devoting a steadfast energy to patriotic improvements and the conquest of adverse circumstances.

Chapter 8

First Glimpse of Texas

After a delay of nearly two weeks in our departure for Texas, the moment at length arrived for going on board the steamship *Globe*, bound for Brazos Island, at the mouth of the Rio Grande, by way of Indianola and Galveston.

I dreaded starting, and, as the last moment approached, clung to the bare comforts of a hotel in a strange city, in preference to embarking on the treacherous sea that lay between us and our destination.

The ship was an old disabled shell that had been already condemned as unsafe, and in the trip following the one which landed us safely was stranded, and went to pieces on a sand-bar, all the crew and passengers perishing, the captain alone barely escaping with his life. He clung to a spar until he lost his consciousness, when, as he neared the shore, a propitious wave dashed him up high and dry on the beach, where he was found. He told me afterwards that death would have been preferable to the well intentioned but agonizing process that was adopted to bring him to life—namely, that of emptying the salt water from his mouth by holding him suspended by the feet, and letting it pour out gradually!

The commander, Captain Thompson, was a splendid specimen of the rough and fearless sailor, a genuine hero of the sea, bold, skilful, a thorough seaman in appearance as well as in mind and soul, with "a soft heart under a rough jacket." His nights at sea were sleepless with watchfulness, and a bare bench on the hurricane deck his only couch.

The shores of the Gulf of Mexico, and its myriads of rocks, shoals, and sand-bars, were as familiar to him as the shifting nature of the latter could make them.

In the past year he has found an untimely grave under these treacherous waters. During a dreadful storm his ship went down, not a soul living to tell where or how.

Our sail down the Mississippi from New Orleans was spent on deck, and was rather pleasant, but towards night, when we got into the Gulf, the ship began to toss among the short sharp waves, and I was shown to the "ladies' cabin," where a shelf a foot wide was pointed out as my bed. Affairs began to assume an aspect anything but pleasant. I was too sick to sit up, yet could not reconcile myself to the idea of the shelf, but increasing sickness left no alternative. I closed my eyes to shut out the scene of dreadful squalor and confusion around, which sickened the very soul.

Families of emigrants lay about on piles of trunks and boxes, all blessed with numerous young children, who cried, screamed, and were sea-sick incessantly. I never can forget that wretched night. I seemed to lie in a trance, wondering if I was myself or someone else, so unlike was the scene to anything my imagination had previously pictured. It seemed a little glimpse of Pandemonium! The next morning I was removed, half dead, to the captain's room on deck, in a state of wretchedness more mental than physical, the stewardess with really kind feelings remarking, as she assisted me, that I "was like a young bear with all my troubles yet to come!"

It is a great era in our lives when we first begin to realize that *life is earnest, life is real*! The feelings of relief were overwhelming on obtaining possession of the unpretending little apartment which was kindly proffered for the rest of the voyage, far away from all those dreadful fellow-passengers.

After a sail of three days, we stopped at Galveston, Texas, one of the principal ports of the State; here we put off a large portion of our passengers, who were emigrating into the interior.

The main object of emigration to this State is of course for agricultural purposes. There are a very superior class of emigrants pouring into this portion of Texas, from the older States, tempted hither by the rich, luxurious, easily-cultivated soil of this well-named garden of the South-West.

Too much cannot be said of the temptations of settling here; it is only in the south-western portion, on the borders of the Rio Bravo del Norte, or the Rio Grande, that the country seems stricken by a blight, and the vegetation becomes meagre and scanty beyond belief.

We stopped for twenty-four hours at Galveston, and a cessation from sea-sickness, combined with a comparatively cool, pleasant day, made us hail with pleasure the idea of spending it on shore.

The country presented a flat sameness of aspect, and the town a growing appearance, in spite of the signs of *newness* that pervaded it; frame houses and cottages, surrounded by gardens, evidently just laid out; streets regularly marked off into blocks; some good stores, and quite an extensive hotel, with churches of several denominations, form the foundation of a city that promises a fine and rapid development. We arrived from the ship at the hotel just in time for dinner, and were quite surprised at the unwonted display of table-napkins and turtle soup—two unlooked-for luxuries! Experience soon proved that the former were an especial compliment to the fair sex, who all over Texas are regarded with great honour and consideration. A gentleman, uninitiated in the customs of the country, asked for a napkin, and was informed by a likely yellow boy, "Only provided for ladies, sir."

I noticed several of these honoured ladies at table, arrayed in the tasteful costume of black barege over white, and enormous coloured breast-pins; their toilets reminded me very strongly of the baboon's sister in nursery tales, described as wearing "a dark black frock, and green glass breastpin." None of them, however, excited my spontaneous admiration.

After dinner was over I went to my room for a *siesta*, and

while there, amused myself reading some of the printed rules by which the house was regulated. To assist those whose business it is to render comfortable the travelling public, I will copy one or two of them—*viz.* "Gents requested not to spit on the walls!" also to "Keep their boots off the bed clothes!" I hope I shall not shock any one's refinement beyond recovery by repeating these regulations, but as they were there in print, it must be that "beings do exist," to whom such warnings are deemed necessary!

I amused myself after dinner by conversing with a crowd of young, round-eyed, woolly-headed darkies, whose teeth shone like rows of ripe Indian corn on the cob, and who, in spite of being as wild and timid as prairie hens, were induced by a small bribe to pour out in chorus some of the sweetest music I ever listened to. Their clear, fresh, untutored voices, blended in perfect harmony as they recounted, in spirited verse, an exciting raccoon hunt in better time than the best drilled choruses I had ever heard.

An exquisite ear for music seems to be the peculiar gift of the negro. They were the property of an old Virginia planter, who had sold his plantation in his native state, and with his sons and sons' sons, and their united families, slaves, and household property, were emigrating to Eastern Texas, to settle on the Brazos river, where he had bought land, and was going to found a new home for himself and his descendants. The whole family came with us from New Orleans in the *Globe*. One day I sat near the old father on deck, and struck by his venerable patriarchal appearance, and quaintness of manners, for my private edification entered into conversation with him. He gave me a great deal of valuable information in regard to the land to which he was bound, and finally asked "Misses, whar was you raised?" I told him in New York.

"It's an awful sinful place," he groaned out, "and was your man raised thar too?"—leaving me very much in doubt whether he thought there could be any future hope of salvation for a sinful mortal "raised" in this modern Sodom!

CHAPTER 9

Galveston, Texas

Towards sunset of the afternoon that we passed in Galveston, a light wagon and a pair of mustang ponies were provided for us, as this flourishing settlement even boasts of a livery stable, so far has civilization advanced.

They gave us the best "turn out" they had. Officers of the army, being the representatives of government, receive the most uniform courtesy and respect all over the South and West.

We first drove through the town. About the whole place there seems to hang a shade of melancholy, which may be imaginary, and in reality unconnected with it, but it is with involuntary thankfulness that I say "my lot has been cast in more pleasant places." There is but little animation in the streets, and we can almost imagine ourselves in a settlement of exiles, so few signs of life are to be seen. However, we often judge of a place by the tone of our minds while there, and if these feelings cannot be laid aside, it is hardly a fair test.

We leave the town behind, and crossing about a mile of *chaparral* or prairie land, reach the beach; a beach that throws that of Newport, and others that we have seen, far, far into the shade. It is twice their width, and can be driven on for a day, without meeting with any impediment. The only marks of life we see are an occasional fisherman's temporary hut or shed, on that part in near vicinity to the town; and further on, swarms of wild ducks, cranes, and other kinds of wild fowl, as well as clusters of mammoth turtles, in which way we easily accounted for the soup at dinner. They lay basking in the hot sand, apparently enjoying life excessively in their own way.

How meagre, how insignificant, do all the seaside scenes painted on memory seem, in comparison to this vast and apparently interminable extent of wave-beaten sand with its glorious breakers, and their sad eternal moanings. The mustang ponies seem inspired to do their best, and go like the wind, on, on, miles and miles, and jet before us apparently the same vast extent of beach, the same breakers, the same flock of storks, wetting their long beaks at the water's brink, startled by our unwonted intrusion on the solitudes, so long alone devoted to them, their predecessors, and the murmurs of the "sad sea wave"—on, on, nothing but grandeur, sublimity, and God—not a sound of humanity.

Sermons and essays are not half as beneficial in their effects as sermons and lessons born of a strange wild scene like this. The sky, the sand, the "wild sea foam," the salt *chaparral* stretching in the opposite direction over the flat lands, are all that the eye finds to rest upon, except the delicate shells and seaweeds that lay strewn in profusion on the beach, toys that the wearied mermaids have cast aside after having wreathed them for pastime in their dripping locks.

At last the sun goes down beyond the sea, . and then in its full beauty rises the moon. Round, full, and beautiful, it rises with a peculiar beauty on the scene we have just described, casting no shadows, for there are no rocks or uneven ground to foster them. It lights the sand, and tinges the waves with silver, as our horses turn their heads homewards. We were very loath to go, and confess to having "on this occasion only" felt very sentimental under the influence of so much beauty, but *è dolce far niente* is most potently realized in moonlight on a southern sea, and makes a little weakness of this kind the more excusable! We will even confess to having been guilty, in the recesses of our own heart, of quoting some poetry in reference to

Those melancholy tears,
Which come when all most bright. appears,

And hold their strange and secret power
Even on pleasure's golden hour.

The sea, scarce murmuring, slept in peace,
Though full of glory bright as noon,
Which through the clouds—a silvery fleece—
Gushed down from the resplendent moon.
Melted in blue the distant flood,
Like jewels gleamed the sparkling sand.
Oh, what in such a silent night
Will through the human bosom throng,
Was never felt by day's broad light,
Was never told in earthly song.
A breath, mysterious, seems to creep
From Heaven upon the tranquil air
A vision o'er the soul to sweep,
'Tis half a smile and half a tear.

It seemed a place to linger in forever, but had this wish been gratified, we fear a speedy reaction would have taken place from this quite high-flown state of enthusiasm, and in time we should have longed for a human habitation, and to see the wild clucks in a pate, as well as many other small items of civilized life. That evening we left Galveston, with a glimpse of its melancholy beauties impressed on the pages of memory, like the trace of a sad and misty dream. At earliest dawn next morning we set sail, and at noon landed at Indianola, where we put off the remainder of our passengers. But few ever go further south in Texas, unless they go on especial business, or by orders of government.

Those unconnected with the latter, or with mercantile houses, seldom find their way there. The passengers for Indianola, and their numerous articles of property, were conveyed to the shore, some distance, in small boats, as, from the peculiar formation of the harbour, it is perilous for ships to enter in. Two more days at sea brought our old, leaky vessel in sight of the island of "Brazos St. Jago" (the arm of St. James), and found us most perilously lodged on a dangerous sand-bar in sight of land, where the vestiges of wrecks around seemed to warn us of what might be our fate, and of the death and destruction that looked us in the face. For six hours we lay in the breakers, with the calm blue, sunlit heavens, smiling down upon us, singular accompaniments for a wreck at sea, and yet we knew well that half the devastations around us had taken place under the same circumstances, and not in the midnight storm or under a clouded sky.

The waves, as if from a whirlpool beneath, dashed upon the ship, striking us fearfully each time against the bar, producing a terrible shock, that seemed like warning from heaven of coming fate. The captain and crew laboured most manfully at their duties, but every other voice was hushed with eager anxiety. The scene around inspired anything but hope of reaching land in safety, and assistance of small boats from the shore experience had often proved impossible. The sea around the vessel moaned "like a monster pained." We sat all these hours on the deck, mechanically watching the sea gulls dipping their wings in the water, and the porpoise as it gave a leap through the air to plunge again, in an instant, into the wave.

When death comes face to face with us unexpectedly, no matter what our horror of it may be, it is strange how indifferently we can look it in the face. During these frightful hours we traced with a glass countless wrecks that lay around. From the bar on which we lay to the shore the water was shallow, and only navigable for small boats. The harbour is filled with bars, which are continually shifting their position. This peculiarity is what renders it so perilous, and causes so many lives to be sacrificed in sight of land. Every imaginable vestige of wreck lay around, from the giant mast of some enormous ship to that of the smallest trading schooner.

All this gave to the barren, sandy shores, an air of gloom and desolation that words cannot describe. Our few fellow-passengers awaited with us in earnest watching to see what would come next. My Irish Abigail alone broke silence, by ejaculations to the Virgin, in a brogue which was a painful jar to every one's feelings, and had I died there it would have been as a sincere and disgusted Know Nothing!

Towards afternoon, when the excitement of hope had been subdued by the almost certainty of our worst fears being realized—with one bound and a loud glad shout of exultation, we were pushed across the bar, and at last safely cast anchor inside the harbour. In her next voyage, the *Globe* went to pieces on this same sand-bar, not a soul on board, except the captain, escaping. It now forms another vestige of a wreck to add new dreariness to this gloomy scene.

The small boats were launched, and we were soon landed on the government docks of Brazos Island, where are a number of large wooden buildings, containing ammunition and various government stores of provisions, clothing, &c., to be forwarded to answer demands from the various military stations on the river above. The quartermaster and his family reside here, and we stayed at his house. That afternoon we spent with him in a rowboat fishing for our supper; we caught a number of blue-fish, and of course cat-fish, as they are the especial luck of all amateur fishermen! We caught nothing different from what we have at the north.

Towards night as we went homewards over the moonlit waters, the cool breeze from the sea amply rewarded us for our unwonted exertions. That evening we sat on the *piazza* and saw the lights glimmering from Point Isabel, which lay directly opposite us on the Texas shore. It will be remembered as the scene of some of General Taylor's most important operations. It contains a few houses around Fort Polk, a field-work thrown up by General Taylor's troops, at the commencement of the war. Between Point Isabel and Brownsville is an overland route of about twelve miles. Shell Island and Palm Island, both occupied by a few inhabitants, lay before us in the sea; Brazos Island looks like a bleak, barren sand-bank on a pretty extensive scale.

In the year 1845, before Texas became a State of the Union, the Mexican government passed a law, that no one should attempt to settle here, as on several occasions, when such attempts had been made, a terrific storm had suddenly sprung up, and, dashing on the shore, had swept away every vestige of its inhabitants and their property, without leaving a trace behind of human habitation. It is now many years since such a storm has taken place, so that they have almost entirely passed from the memory of the present inhabitants of these regions.

Government has run quite a risk in braving a repetition of one of these terrible and devastating storms. It may lead to a too tardy regret. The present limited population are principally the *employés* of government at the store-houses, and fishermen who supply the Brownsville market with bass, red and blue-fish, and an inferior kind of oyster, which is nevertheless regarded as a very great delicacy in the absence of others.

I was very much amused at a new species of hotel that I saw there; it was formed of the wrecked hull of an enormous ship that had been cast ashore in a storm, and was firmly wedged in the sand. It had been repaired and rendered weather-proof by the mud and mortar generally made use of for building- purposes in these primitive regions. A bar-room and eating-room formed the principal apartments, with several sleeping-rooms of limited area adjoining, which were the accommodations of the boarders. It was kept by an old woman and her pretty little granddaughter about twelve years old, who was receiving an education to fit her for the responsible situation of bar-maid to this "Hotel (*vraiment*) Texan." We passed one afternoon and night on Brazos Island, and the next day started for Fort Brown, adjoining the town of Brownsville, Texas.

Chapter 10

Brazos St. Jago

At ten o'clock the next morning the government carriage or ambulance was at the door, and, bidding farewell to our host, we again resumed our journey. The day was warm, but a cool breeze came from the sea, and the sun kindly shut out its hottest rays from us by a screen of clouds. The first part of the drive lay along the seaboard of Brazos Island; no rocks, nor the smallest traces of vegetation could be seen in the hot sand; there was nothing to vary the monotony of the scene but vestiges of wrecks of all descriptions, remains of ships and schooners, that when gaily launched, brightly painted, and colours streaming, were looked upon with pride by their commander and crew, who little thought they would, ere long, be utterly disabled, at the mercy of tempestuous winds, cast on the bleak shores of a barren island, or stranded on the treacherous sand-bar.

Frequently were we compelled to turn aside from our path to avoid some mammoth blackened mast that lay imbedded in the sand, impeding our way. The horses dragged for several miles, slowly and wearily, through the heavy sands, till we came to the creek "Boca Chica" (little mouth), which separates Brazos Island from the main land. Here the horses were taken from the ambulance, which was then towed across the creek by the flat-boat, that served for a ferry; it then returned for the horses, and finally for the passengers, making three tedious trips, while I sat on a dressing-case, in the sand, patiently watching the operation.

The flat-boat could not come quite up to the dry land, so

there were about twenty yards of shallow water to be passed before we could get to it. To my amazement I soon found myself being borne through the air like a baby in the arms of a great stalwart Texan (he being knee-deep in the water), until safely lodged in the boat, on a large Mexican *poncho* that their gallantry had provided. The creek was over a quarter of a mile wide, and was a good deal swollen at this season by recent rains. When we arrived at the other side we were obliged to wait there a while to rest the horses.

We went into a kind of *rancho,* or hut, to sit down. It was the home of the boatman and his wife, who resided here, and the only house for miles around; it appeared very lonely, even to a transient guest, being on the banks of the creek, with nothing but sand and water in sight. The interior was quite spacious, and was divided into apartments by rough canvass or sailcloth curtains. All the surroundings, however, to an eye unaccustomed to "roughing it," bore an aspect of misery and abject suffering. When on our way home we again stopped here, this wayside hut, with a roof over it, appeared (comparatively speaking) really a comfortable abode, we had seen so many worse ones.

In a conversation with the woman who lived here, she told her history (which was but slightly more eventful than that of Canning's Knife-Grinder)!

The "halcyon days" of her youth had been passed principally on the canal. Since that she had lived in all parts of the Western States, and finally had reached this barren spot, on the confines of civilization. She bore the traces of some former beauty; her eyes were very sad, and so was her smile. I asked her if she was not lonely, she said that peace was enough to satisfy her, and she had that where she was. Her chief occupation was raising chickens for the Brownsville market. She showed me a brood of fifty, with one old hen, all crowded in a bandbox, and kept on a shelf, to keep them from running in the creek, she said. By the aid of plenty of meal and a scanty supply of light and air, she assured me she raised the fattest chickens in market! but I should not have cared to eat any of these extra plethoric or dropsical poultry!

By the time the investigation of this natural phenomenon was finished, our horses were rested and at the door awaiting us. We bid our hostess farewell, and proceeded on our way.

From this point we struck a north-westerly direction towards Brownsville, crossing a beautiful *chaparral*, which, owing to an accidental irrigation from the overflow of the river above, formed a spot of verdure but seldom seen in this region of country. It was thick with flowering shrubs and wild flowers. Each scraggy, ebony tree lodged in its branches myriads of brilliant tropical birds, whose sweet-toned melodies filled the soft air that floated around us, with music. Another hour's drive took us to the borders of the Rio Grande or Rio Bravo del Norte, a still, monotonous stream, that flowed sluggishly along, its muddy waters giving, however, a refreshing sensation to the traveller on its almost invariably parched and arid banks.

The first impressions of this river reminded me of the descriptions I had read and imagined of Egypt and the Nile. It only wanted a few swarthy, turbaned men, and a sphinx or two, to complete the illusion.

As we left the banks of the river (which, in its winding course, struck far away from our more direct road to Brownsville), we came on to the ground which was the scene of the battle of Palo Alto, situated on a tract which nature seemed designedly to have thrown up for the purposes of a drill ground. This formation is not, however, as conspicuous in this region of country as it might be in another place; for the whole surface of the land is laid out in low, sandy ridges, the vegetation stinted, and the soil scanty. The cactus and other plants indigenous and peculiar to a sandy soil, grow in luxuriant beauty.

Occasionally relics of the battle are picked up, but there remain few traces to tell of "war's alarms." The oriole boldly lights on the low flowering bushes, knowing no fear in these rarely interrupted solitudes, where the sounds of the wilderness alone break the stillness of the air. The contrast of this peaceful scene with the previously conceived idea of this famous battlefield was very striking. It had been associated with the sound of booming guns, gallant charges, and groans of wounded and dying men.

Many that I had known, treading with martial step the romantic plain of West Point, had hero found a soldier's grave, among the unforgotten dead. The high beating pulse and earnest aspirations of early manhood stilled forever, in an instant, by the shot of some cowardly Mexican, who probably shuddered with fear as he pulled his trigger—for they are a nation of poltroons, and more afraid of their own firearms than anyone would readily believe. How many have thus

Poured their life-blood freely out pro bono publico

with the simple satisfaction of dying in the discharge of duty; while, too, many a neglected mound, on distant spots like this, is all that remains of those—

The young and strong, who cherished
Noble longings for the strife,
By the roadside fell and perished.

It seems almost a disgrace to think of the many forgotten graves of brave and noble men that lie scattered everywhere. The glory conferred by them on their country seems to demand some better return. The blood-stained hills and valleys of our land are the ruby jewels in the crown of her greatness. And if we fail to mark those spots where heroes fall with tablets that tell of their gallant deeds, it is not only wronging them, but wronging generations yet unborn, by allowing them to forget how precious the purchase-money that bought their freedom.

Our horses paused here to allow us to take luncheon, which, when it came to be unpacked, consisted of a cold beefsteak and bread, wrapped in a newspaper; anything but a tempting repast, and, although famishing with hunger, I politely but firmly declined participating in it.

About three miles before we came to Fort Brown we passed a deep ravine, the scene of the battle of Resaca de la Palma (the field of palms), which could not have taken its name from any of these trees, as there was not even one specimen to be seen. It was here that General Taylor achieved his second victory over the Mexicans, under General Arista, in the late war. The sensations here were a repetition of the above, so it is needless to recapitulate.

When we are hungry we grow less enthusiastic, and even patriotism cools down to a mere matter of fact sentiment.

We saw several ranches in the distance, but none near enough to form a very definite idea of them or their belongings.

Chapter 11

Fort Brown

Soon we drove in sight of Fort Brown, and up the principal street of Brownsville to the gates of the garrison. The aspect of this curious, half-breed town, was very novel. It is what they call in Texas "quite a settlement." A mixed population of Americans and Mexicans formed a contrast at once striking and amusing.

On the one hand the red brick stores, and white frame shops and buildings of every description, bore the marks of inevitable progress, or go-aheadativeness, otherwise called "manifest destiny;" while the rudely constructed huts, or *hackals*, composed of rustic straw work, or mud bricks called *adobes*, in which there is generally but one apartment, where frequently are found live generations living together, eking out an indolent existence on a mild diet of ground corn, eggs, and milk, exhibited unmistakable evidence of a vanishing people, who in a few years will know no nationality.

These Mexicans lead a truly primitive life, reminding us of "shepherd days" in young world's history.

In one of the huts, built on four posts, with thatched straw walls, I witnessed on one occasion, with mingled horror and amusement, quite a new phase in barber-*ism*! It could not be called hair-dressing, yet might be regarded as a peculiar species of shampooing.

An old crone seated on a wooden bench, was cleansing the locks of a small child, while a young girl performed the same kindly offices for the old woman—the whole party talking and laughing merrily.

Further description, or even a shade more minuteness in detail, would be impossible. Sufficient to say, the performance had more vitality connected with it than is usually displayed by Mexicans.

Vermin are the scourge of this country, and cleanliness certainly not one of its virtues. This portion of the world may be set down as the birthplace of the flea; those found in other parts are merely occasional wanderers from this, their native land! Here they roam at large, the torment, *par excellence*, of the human race, in consequence of which carpets are eschewed, as they are apt to furnish a resort for scores of fleas, as well as other vermin of the country.

Cane furniture, matting, and the indispensable mosquito bar, are the only articles in general use; anything more elegant seldom reaches here, and is not required.

We found at Brownsville quite a respectable, well educated class of Americans, who gave an entertainment while we were there, in honour of certain strangers in town. The mayor called to invite the officers of the garrison of Fort Brown, and their families, to the *soirée* to be given at "the Gem," the principal café of the place. Of course we accepted the invitation, went at nine o'clock, and found the affair had commenced already.

A fine band of stringed instruments, and a certain air of deference and respect in the manners of the men, were something I had not expected to find. The waltzing was very graceful. Several Spanish ladies from the old Mexican city of Matamoras were present, who seemed to swim in the graceful, languid motion of the *deux temps*, as if they had never heard of the hopping of the polka and *redowa*, which rather frantic style of dancing certainly seems better adapted to the Jardin Mabille, or some *grisettes'* ball, than to the dame *comme il faut*.

Wallflowers are an unknown shrub in this part of the country; the men have too much gallantry to allow them to flourish, even if accidentally transplanted here from colder climes.

I had once doubted the existence of those mythical beings

called "nature's noblemen," but my stay in Texas relieved my mind from all uncertainty on the subject, for I found no lack of polish and courtesy, although the country is so newly settled.

The site now occupied by the government grounds of Fort Brown belonged formerly to the estate of a Spanish nobleman, and had been in his family for years. Consequently some fine trees are growing in the neighbourhood, as it was once an exquisite garden, filled with plants and irrigated from the Rio Grande, by moans of stone aqueducts, now falling into decay. Traces of a beautiful artificial lake, with an island in its centre, still remain, and also a ruined summer-house, with luxuriant vines creeping wherever they can find a support to cling to, as the pillars that they once clambered over have probably long ere this lighted a fire, to cook some *ranchero's* meal, or floated down the sullen waters of the Rio Grande.

In 1848 Brownsville contained but two house's, or rather shanties; two years after, it had four thousand inhabitants, was laid out into streets, with a number of brick buildings, and a fine market-house, with a large public hall above it. It is duly incorporated, and now has a mayor and other municipal officers, and a weekly newspaper.

Its population has not very materially increased since 1850, owing to the unsettled state of the frontier, from the Indians and filibuster warfare. A considerable trade is carried on with the interior of Mexico, and in time of disturbance smuggling is practised to a great extent.

The rush of fortune-hunters to California gave so wide a vent to the enterprising, that it prevented the increase of the population of Brownsville that would otherwise have taken place.

Thirty miles east of the town is a lake, from which large quantities of salt are annually obtained.

In 1852 when we were there, there was no church, and but one preacher. This individual was a wandering Presbyterian, who after having collected an ample subscription from the people, for the purpose of building a church, invested it in a parsonage, built on a lot of his own ground! and after safely lodging in it his wife and a dozen or more of his pious offspring, began making preparations for another collection, to build the church. This time, however, the people of Brownsville, seeing that he acted so entirely on the principle of *charity beginning at home*, were more wary, and the church remains unbuilt to this day. I have since heard that the Episcopal church has sent a minister there.

We were detained several weeks in Brownsville on account of the non-arrival of the *Corvette* (the government steamer), and during that time received every kindness and hospitality. The further you remove from civilization, the more warm-hearted the persons you meet seem, and hospitality, like contentment, gives charms, even to "a dinner of herbs." This is easily accounted for. In a large community, there are so many calls on our sympathy and good will, that, naturally, they cannot be responded to as heartily as in a place out of the world, where such demands are more rare.

We made a good many excursions about the country. One day we crossed the river, and spent a day at Matamoras. This place is associated with the siege of Fort Brown, during the Mexican war. Its old stone dwellings, and cathedral, whose cracked chimes float daily on the evening and morning air, with its heavy masonry and antiquated air, seem to bear us back to past centuries when the Spaniards brought from gorgeous Spain some of the attributes of regal grandeur, and planted them in the wilderness of a foreign land. Members of some of the noblest families of Spain founded houses here, whose descendants greatly pride themselves on their long line of ancestors, and the antiquity of their family reminiscences.

The present race of Spanish-Americans have lost almost all the fire of their native land, and form a nation which by itself will probably never attain a very proud eminence in the world's history. Annexation to our union is all that can elevate them, although the advantage would be greatly on their side, as it would not add. either to the glory or material advantage of Uncle Sam. Petty revolutions furnish them with an apparently unwearying excitement, and the consequence is, an utter lack of all progress, and a general aspect of desolation and decayed splendour. The men are generally a diminutive race, and to a refined mind there is something almost repulsive in their dark, swarthy, unintellectual beauty. The upper class of women, though not strictly speaking beautiful, have a certain indescribable charm; a dreamy, soft, subdued, almost languid manner, covering an enthusiasm almost startling when roused.

This anomalous combination produces an effect at once pleasing and the contrary. We feel how necessary a high cultivation of the mind is to a union so fascinating and so defective. For beyond accompanying herself on the mandolin, as she sings the national ditties of Spain, and embroidering the exquisite needlework of Mexico, she is utterly devoid of either moral or literary culture. While at Matamoras, we saw the funeral procession of the resident Spanish Consul, to which the American officers had received a formal and courteous invitation; many of them were present. lie was of the Roman faith, and his funeral services were attended with all the pomp and forms of that church.

The carriage that we were in drew up to the side of the road, as the procession passed in solemn silence, the only sounds the low chanting of the priests and the tram]) of the feet of the funeral train. The priests came first, in full regalia, bearing the host, followed by boys in white and crimson attire, holding lighted torches, and burning incense; then came the coffin, borne on the shoulders of six men, and covered with a heavy black velvet pall, with deep gold fringe. On the top lay the *chapeau*, sword, and sash of its occupant, with other insignia of his office (which latter among these people are neither few nor rare). The mourners followed in close vicinity to the coffin, and then the citizens, each bearing a long waxen taper, to be lighted at the grave during the service.

The fat shaven *padres* seemed to be enjoying vastly the impression they were producing on their ignorant but admiring audience, and (begging the pardon of the holy Roman Catholic Church) a more dissolute, carnal, gambling, jolly set of winebibbers do not exist in any portion of the world than the Mexican priests of the present day. In every village of importance they are found, ruling the ignorant peasantry with the strong sway of superstition and dread. These men are at times well educated, and very agreeable, amusing companions, in spite of their wickedness. They differ widely from the original race of priests, who were among the foremost in bringing religion and civilization into the country.

In fact, the earliest records we have of the history of Mexico and Texas are derived from those remarkable men, half priest, half soldier, who after aiding in the subjugation of the Aztecs, spread themselves almost single-handed over a vast extent of country, uninhabited save by numerous tribes of savages, whose very existence was unknown to each other. Led on by visions as brilliant as those of Cortez, fired equally by religious zeal and ambition, these modern crusaders braving danger with more than military ardour, and meeting death with the martyr's enthusiasm, with their numbers diminished and still decreasing, pressed on until they penetrated into the heart of the continent, where for centuries the wild idolator had offered sacrifice on the altar of an unknown God.

Descending the water courses to the Gulf of Mexico, they sought with the cross in one hand, and the sword in the other, to colonize the nomadic tribes that roamed at large over the wide prairies of Texas. The history of their proceedings is full of interest, although the records are few and limited in detail. Time and again their efforts were frustrated, and the daring adventurers paid to their enterprise the forfeit of their lives.

Occasionally a straggling survivor found his way back to Mexico, after passing through every description of danger, travelling solitary and on foot over hundreds of miles of prairie. Their mournful tidings, however, served but to increase the ardour for conquest. Success seemed at length to crown these continued efforts, and a number of flourishing missions were eventually established in the valley of the upper Rio Grande, and formed the nucleus of what are now considerable towns. These missions were generally under the supervision of the priests, one of whom attended to the religious ceremonies, while the other collected the Indians, and instructed them in agriculture, the use of implements, &c.

In these tasks they were assisted by parties of already civilized Indians, who had accompanied them from Mexico. At first the converts were supported by the mission, which in return received their labour. As soon as they were deemed competent to provide for themselves, a portion of ground was allotted to them, and in this way a village sprang up around each mission. For several years these little communities remained undisturbed, each year adding to their number, and increasing their resources. Yet, while reposing in fancied security, an unseen storm was gathering around them.

The wily savages of the plains, true to the instinct of their untamable and rapacious natures, only waited for a fitting opportunity to sweep down upon the settlements and annihilate them. Not content with plundering them of everything they could carry away, they ruthlessly murdered all who could be found, and the missions were for a time abandoned. We cannot fail to regret that so little of the heroic and religious zeal of these first priests remains to inspire their followers.

Just outside of the town of Brownsville are the grounds of the garrison of Fort Brown, the spot from whence General Taylor bombarded Matamoras. Its well kept fences, and regularly placed barracks and buildings, with the vine-covered cottages that form the officers' quarters, add in no small degree to the beauty and importance of Brownsville; while the daily guard-mountings, parades, and drills, and the accompanying military music, add greatly to the feelings of safety and importance of its citizens.

While at Fort Brown I saw a soldier from the ranks drummed out of the service for theft. It was a very novel and amusing sight. He had his head shaved, and his military coat, hat, and accoutrements taken from him—his blue pantaloons, with the red stripe of the artillery, he alone retained to show his former calling. At evening parade he was called in front of the ranks, and publicly dismissed, the officer of the day reading his crime and its penalty, aloud, in full. He was then obliged to walk three times around the parade-ground, with the corporal and sergeant of the guard following him closely with bayonets pointed downward, the fifer and two drummers following, playing "right merrily" the tune of "Poor Old Soldier, I hope the devil won't catch you," a gay, mocking air reserved especially for occasions of this kind. He put on a regular Jack Sheppard or Dick Turpin swagger, and in passing the commanding officer's quarters, shouted out to a group there assembled for a subscription for a wig.

A prick from the two bayonets soon put him in mind of his flagrant breach of respect, but it did not seem to cure him, as on his last tour he called to the orderly of the day, who stood with military bearing and a wooden face, "Goodbye, Tom! God bless you, my son!" The orderly's face became still more wooden and unresponsive at this remark, as in duty bound, and a severe prick from the guard produced another strong reminder of duty. At the gate of the garrison he was ejected, and went off probably to buy himself a wig!—while the guard marched rapidly back to the guard-house, followed by the fifer and the drummers playing the tune of "The Dashing White Sergeant," a sound inspiriting enough to give the soldier fresh strength on the weariest march, or call the most lagging recruit to his post.

Chapter 12

The Rio Bravo del Norte

The *Corvette* finally arrived, and after stopping a few days at Brownsville, prepared to start again on its return trip, up the Rio Grande. We were the only passengers on board. The accommodations were very fine, as there were only two state rooms, and they four times the usual size, and quite sumptuously furnished.

We spent four days in our sail up the river, which runs in a singularly serpentine course; at times, the windings form almost a complete circle. Sand-bars were very numerous, and (to use a technical local phrase) we "*stuck*" a number of times on the way, going through the process of several hours' tugging and pushing each time before we were able to continue our voyage, which, had it not been for its novelty, might have proved tedious.

About half way up the river, we came to a settlement, on the American side, called Edinburgh. A thieving Scotchman had built a house here, and patriotically called it after his native place, which he had probably left in a hurry!

A few Mexicans have clustered around him, find it is now a stopping-place for the occasional flat-boats that go up and down the river, with lumber, provisions, &c.

The only notice we took of its existence as a city was by flinging a package of papers ashore from the mail bag as we passed it.

Not far above this, Ave were suddenly alarmed by the dreadful cry of "the Camanches! the Camanches!" and a momentary pang of terror was felt by the stoutest heart on board.

Their rifles were aimed at our "great canoe with pinions," and several harmless shots penetrated different objects on deck.

We returned the fire, and most fortunately heard no more from them. They were probably bound on other errands of destruction and death.

The story of the dreadful crimes which they practise on the inhabitants of this region will form a fearful page in history. There could not be a blacker record of infamy and rapaciousness. The Camanche Indian possesses no vestige of the noble traits attributed to the red men of the north west. At the best, he enjoys the mere intelligence, or rather instincts, of the brute; these instincts are all that guide him. He is bloody, brutal, licentious, and an innate thief. Civilization will probably never reach him, as his feelings towards the white men are those of implacable hatred. Their blood he demands, and takes every occasion to obtain it. With the terrible sound of his name, the Mexican mother strikes terror to the soul of her wayward child. In fact, he may be looked upon as "the black man in the coal-hole" of more civilized lands. Actual extermination seems to suggest itself as the only remedy against this scourge. Nothing less will render many portions of the State of Texas a safe abode for white settlers.

The Camanche's food is principally raw meat of the animals killed in the hunt, which diet probably renders more formidable his ferocious nature. The tribe resides further north than the Rio Grande, but roving parties are continually coming down for depredation and murder.

They are wonderful horsemen, more in their natural element on a horse's back than anywhere else. An Indian child is put on horseback before it can walk, with a cord around the horse's neck, and taught to guide it with its feeble strength, more adroitly than can be readily imagined. The women ride astride, and are quite as fearless riders as the men. Their favourite sport is to lasso wild horses, which they do with great expertness. A band of mounted Camanches in full chase after a drove of wild horses, with their manes flying in the wind, is said to be an intensely exciting sight. The Indian lassos his horse, jumps on the wild, restive creature's back, and remains there till he is in a measure broken in.

They say, among the Indians, that in breaking a horse's spirit they break his heart, and he does not live long; consequently, they always endeavour to catch colts, as "breaking in" has always been found to be more successful during the tender period of youth than in maturer years, in human beings as well as wild horses!

Horse-stealing from the Mexicans is an important branch of their business. He who steals the greatest number of horses is regarded as the greatest man in the tribe. After all, life is made up of conventionalities, and what is honourable with one nation is dishonour with another. If for horses we read dollars, I fear we should have a peculiar fact in regard to more enlightened communities!

Government has, at different times, organized parties, and sent them up to the principal camping grounds of the tribe. But the great *sachem* and chief men have disclaimed all connexion with these marauding parties, placing them in the light of filibusters, beyond their control. An astute idea of theirs, for if we cannot control organized depredations on our neighbours, how can we blame the Indians for wishing to extend their "area of freedom?" My ideas of these savages were acquired from the Texans and Mexicans, of course not from actual contact; yet I cannot refrain from some feelings of sympathy for a people, who are driven from their rightful possessions, and can see, in their ignorance, many excuses for their tiger-like ferocity and bitter hatred of those who they feel have wronged them so sorely.

The night before we arrived at the point of our final destination, the steamer pushed towards the shore, and we tied up for the night at a Mexican *rancho*, as at this point in the river sailing by night was considered dangerous. We ran ashore late in the afternoon, and landed to inspect the immediate vicinity of the country. Taking a road that led from the river's bank in a winding direction through the *chaparral*—a beaten footpath led us on—each side overrun with briers, among them myriads of beautiful wild flowers, "uncultured blossoms of the wilderness," glowing in delicate and varied lines, as they sprung from the sterile and sandy soil, unlooked for traces of a beauty whose spirit seems to linger everywhere—we soon emerged from the tangled brush-wood of the *chaparral*, and came to a cleared spot of some acres in extent. The picture of rural pursuits that here presented itself, was a study for an artist.

Half-a-dozen mud-huts neatly thatched with straw and open sheds attached for culinary purposes, where the kettle hung suspended over a wood fire, in real gipsy fashion, while an old weather-beaten crone bent over, stirring the *pot-au-feu* of *frijoles* that were to make the evening meal.

The men who had returned from the chase or from the fields lay about on the ground, or leaned lazily over the fence, talking to the women who were milking a flock of goats, and some cows that the children had just driven in from their scanty pasturage in the *chaparral*.

One Mexican girl, as she milked her goats, talked and smiled most coquettishly, the while showing her beautiful eyes and teeth to great advantage to a "greaser," who evidently appreciated her charms! His slouched *sombrero* and enormous black moustache, with traces in his dress of the picturesque garb of Spain, produced an exceedingly artistic effect.

The peasant women wear a white *chemisette décolletée*, with short sleeves, and a dark bright-coloured petticoat; they are rather slovenly, and consequently far from attractive, although at a little distance they look well.

A large garden and a good-sized patch of Indian corn, interspersed with melon vines, together with cattle and an enormous flock of barnyard fowls, completed the scene. It took me back in my mind to past centuries that Schiller sings of—

> *The age when the Earth was at play*
> *In the childhood and bloom of creation,*
> *When no grief and no guile the calm shepherd-race knew;*
> *And their life was the absence of care,*

when Chloe and her shepherd swain were the chosen theme of the poet's pen.

The children roamed *"sans culottes"* as usual in this climate, and were very pretty, although it was painfully evident that the institution of Saturday night ablutions, common in all well organized nurseries, was unheard of among these poor little Mexican babies!

The Mexican peasant of the Rio Grande is a character peculiar to that region of country, possessing within himself all the elements of a social existence. He is his own shoemaker and tailor; the leather of his garments and of his sandals is made from the skins of the animals he has himself killed.

He makes his own carts, hewing the wheels out of the solid wood. He makes the plough he uses, which is a sharp-pointed log, with a pole at one end by which it is guided, and one at the other by which it is drawn. To it a pair of oxen are strapped by the horns; sometimes a mule and a cow are yoked together to drag it! His harrow is made of the branch of a tree. The corn is put into the ground and then left to Providence to either ripen or dry up, of which there is an even chance.

After planting he starts out on the prairie to lasso wild horses and cattle, and if he escapes the Camanche, he generally brings home a supply of stock for the ensuing year. He builds his house of straw, reeds, stone and adobes, without either nails or hammer; lingers out his inoffensive peaceful life almost invariably to a good old age; and goes to his grave without knowing or caring anything about the world, except that portion of it which is bounded by the horizon of his own *rancho*.

Chapter 13

Ringgold Barracks

We reached Camp Ringgold on the fourth day, at noon. The arrival of the steamer seemed to be an event that created a great excitement. All the soldiers off duty, and several officers, awaited our landing on the dock. This being the only mode of communication that these exiles have with their kind, the arrival of a mail and newspapers from the world beyond is naturally an important occurrence.

The military post of Ringgold Barracks rose before us on a high sandy bluff, its rows of long, low, whitewashed modern buildings, placed at regular intervals around a level drill ground, in the centre of which rose the flag-staff, with its colours hanging droopingly, unstirred by the sultry air. These buildings were the government store-houses, soldiers' barracks, and officers' quarters; they all reminded me of the house of the foolish man, "who built his foundation upon the sand," all being in a similar plight. There were no signs of vegetation around; not even a blade of grass was to be seen. The sentinels monotonously walking guard gave unmistakable token of a military post.

The deep feeling of relief that our long journey was at length at an end, made me greet with delight the first moment that I landed upon the parched and uninviting sand which composed the bluff upon which the barracks were built. Probably on the principle that "any hut unto a homeless man is welcome," it was with intense pleasure that I took possession of the house assigned to me. Peace and quiet, after the turmoil and excitement of sea-sickness and travelling, seemed what I might at least find here, and I now look back to the year passed in this isolated spot as one full of pleasant recollections.

Each day was filled with new impressions of a new country and new people. Surrounded by those whose intelligence and polish would have been appreciated in the most elegant salons in the world, I can never forget all the kindness and good-will shown to me in Texas both by our officers and the Texans. I never saw a woman while there, except a Mexican peasant or a camp woman. The *abigail* I had taken with me received an offer of marriage while in Brownsville, which (being over thirty-five) she accepted with alacrity, preferring a permanent situation at the head of the establishment of a sentimental blacksmith, to one less certain.

In consequence, I was left to the tender mercies of an African *valet de chambre*, who took the place of *femme de chambre*, to which he had been drilled by some navy officers, whom he accompanied on a cruise in the Mediteranean. He proved himself what in pathetic language might be called the comfort of this period of my life! This faithful negro shone both literally and figuratively in many capacities; he was at once chambermaid, waiter, and housekeeper; and like that faithful Scotchman, Caleb Balderstone, prided himself on keeping up the style of the family! No matter how forlorn the fare, the silver, glass, and china glistened in immaculate purity, and Joseph Williams always, I may say, presided at our board with an untiring grace and clearance of demeanour! A soldier officiated as cook, and with the occasional assistance of a drummer-boy as scullion, divided the labours of the household, with which I never dreamed of interfering.

It was May when we reached there, and we were plunged into a tropical summer, which would have been unendurable had it not been for the delightfully cool nights, when a sea-breeze, full of the fresh aroma of the ocean, would spring up. During the heat of the day, aggravating visions of Newport would at times come across me, but in spite of all inconveniences novelty is so charming that I found a great deal to enjoy in this new land; the climate was very salubrious, and cholera almost unheard of. During the summer months I remained a great deal at home. It was not till the fall that we commenced riding about the country in search of adventure and novelty.

These months passed by rapidly. I amused myself making a kind of Robinson Crusoe collection of pets. By September it consisted of a fawn, two goats, a flock of doves, a brood of chickens, a parrot, four dogs of different kinds, several mocking birds, and some orioles, to say nothing of a tiger cub, of whom I had a mortal fear, who was kept chained, and poked at, and fed on raw meat by our faithful negro, who took these judicious means of taming him!

This small specimen of "a happy family" was kept in a large inclosure in the rear of the house, surrounded by a high fence of interlaced brush-wood, peculiar to Mexican *ranchos*.

In a mounted regiment, blood horses of course abound, but they all had too much spirit to go in harness, although superb under the bit. We could not extend our rides very far from the garrison, on account of the frequent close neighbourhood of the Camanches. The only safe ride was a racecourse just outside of the government grounds. We made many unsuccessful efforts to get a horse that would go in a wagon, and one day heard of a pair that were to be sold, which had been ridden down from Northern Texas across the prairies, and were used up, by being overworked on the road.

Their owner, a rough Texan, now offered them for sale. One died before we got there, and the other! A mere verbal description can never do him justice! Ribs were the chief impression he produced, but his owner said oats and rest would restore him, and he would fatten up, and become a splendid critter! With this vague hope he was purchased for "about five dollars," his owner "reckoned." I did not wonder at the snorting and pawing of the ground (expressive of impatience and disgust) performed by the horse I was sitting, as he came in contact with this miserable specimen of his race, while it took all my strength to hold him in.

The way-worn creature was sent to the garrison that afternoon, but evidently felt the exertion to be too much for his feeble frame. Oats and bran were administered with but small success. For weeks he lingered on, occasionally taking little walks or standing mournfully under the shed which was his stable, looking so sad, so patient, and so motionless, that rows of blackbirds would perch on his sharp backbone, unmolested by the feeble switches of his scanty-tail! Unlike other horses, he did not "feel his oats;" his prime had passed; there was no more "fattening up" for him in this world. That he would never be a "splendid critter" again was evident! He finally died from swallowing a wine-glass! A peculiar death, one of unfrequent occurrence, and worth at least a word of explanation.

A basket of straw, which had been used in packing glass, stood near his shed. He took a mouthful of it, *pour passer le temps*, one sultry morning. A wine-glass remained among it, encased most elaborately in hay (as is the wont of professional packers to encase them). This he recklessly bit at, it got into his throat, and proved the instrument that accomplished his death. Peace be to his veteran bones, for they were many!

Another of my dumb friends to whom I cannot fail to pay the tribute of a few words of remembrance, was—a chicken!—whose benevolence of disposition and kindness of heart elevated him in my eyes for above the level of the humble race to which he belonged. His personal appearance was yellow, delicate, and very bobtailed! his mien was subdued and even melancholy, so much so that he involuntarily reminded me of a young divinity student whom I had known!

An old hen of his acquaintance had a brood of children, one of whom she maltreated, or, to use the technical phrase, "hen-pecked," so that the poor thing, too small to pick for itself, would have been left to die, had not this tender-hearted and philanthropic chicken come to its rescue. He took it literally "under his wing," where it slept at night. He picked food for it, providing it with grasshoppers, spiders, and other delicacies.

One was never to be seen without the other; they presented quite a touching sight, even if they were only chickens.

Their final fate was a sad one! At times our larder was in a deplorable condition, quite bare, without a resource left by which it might be replenished; while on other occasions, when a Mexican would ride into camp with a dozen wild turkeys swung across his saddle, it was quite the opposite. Sometimes an Indian hunter would ride up to the door with a whole deer, even the skin and antlers, and scores of prairie hens, and game of every kind, hanging in the rear. At such times there was nothing to complain of, but at others, if a piece of kid or rabbit, or a few turnips (sold for a *real*, or a shilling apiece), could be obtained, it was looked upon as almost too good fortune to be real.

At one period, which I shall never forget, the quartermaster's stores were reduced to mouldy flour and rancid pork, two luxuries that are not generally very highly appreciated, even by the unfastidious.

A long drought had lowered the river by extensive evaporations, so as to render it unnavigable; and the same cause had parched the country around, making it even more than usually sterile and unproductive.

The steamboat with the monthly supplies of provisions could not get up the river. Starvation seemed staring us in the face. Even *frijoles* (the Mexican bean, an unfailing stand-by) became scarce, and butter, milk, bread, and other such small but necessary items, were utterly unknown to us for weeks. At this period dinner became a dreadful ordeal, it seemed like swallowing a succession of pills; but he would have been a cowardly soldier who complained, when all suffered alike, and the subject of food was one that was dropped by mutual consent!—discussion would only have aggravated the evil.

It was during this time, when sickness and "*les vapeurs noirs*" confined me to the house, that my poor little friend, the chicken and the forlorn little one that he had befriended, were transformed into an ignoble *fricassee*. They were not roasted, out of respect to my feelings, as by their difference of size (which was marked) I might have recognised them! No instinct warned me that I was partaking of my friends. They must have tasted tenderly, if the mind has the influence over the body they say it has.

I was afterwards told the particulars of their fate: As our resources diminished for supplying the table, the eyes of our coloured dependant fixed themselves on this loving pair, who, however, fought manfully and sagaciously for their lives,—three successive days retiring under the house just before the very hour of execution arrived, with an intelligent expression of "no, you don't," on their pointedly expressive faces. Finally, they were cut off while in the arms of Morpheus (if Morpheus admits poultry into those precincts!), and formed the above mentioned dish.

I felt very badly on the following day, when I found that they had been eaten, but was comforted by the thought of how many in a state of famine had been obliged to eat their intimate friends, and even their best fitting boot! It is always best to philosophize. In fact, some of our fates would be unendurable were it not for this wonderful and unfailing panacea.

At last the joyful news arrived that the *Corvette* was a few miles down the river with supplies, but *stuck* in a sand-bar, and the time of its precise arrival consequently very uncertain. Two "gallant sons of Mars" immediately volunteered, and started on horseback to go down the river, and bring me some supplies. They returned towards evening, heavily laden, receiving my gratitude as "ample compensation" for a day's toil. A fine illustration of the word politeness! and quite worthy of record.

Under the most favourable circumstances, the food was flavoured with red ants, which were so thick that it was impossible to eat without devouring them by scores. They tasted something like caraway seed, and were not as disagreeable as a novice might suppose!

The water we drank came from the Rio Grande, and was invariably lukewarm. After straining it, it was kept in a stone jug encased in wet flannel, and suspended by a cord in the air, for the purpose of cooling it as much as possible.

The butter was almost unpalatable from its soft liquid appearance, and was kept in stone jars underground with bricks laid over them. The milk was that of cows and goats, promiscuously milked in the same pail.

The vermin, the famine, hot winds, and dry soil, which caused clouds of dust to fill the sultry air of July and August and lodge on everything, made me begin to think that General Twiggs' advice, that it would be better to remain in New Orleans and keep a thread and needle store than go to Texas, had been quite judicious! However, these evils began to disappear in a measure as the season of fall and winter approached, and our rides became longer and more varied.

CHAPTER 14

Davis's Ranch

About a mile above Ringgold Barracks, on the banks of the Rio Grande, lies the town of "Rio Grande City," until quite recently known as "Davis's Ranch," so called from its founder and present chief magistrate, the Honourable H. Clay Davis, upon the history of whose life it would not be uninteresting, perhaps, to dwell for a moment.

He left his home in Kentucky when quite a boy. His father had been dead some years, and becoming tired of the restraint imposed upon him by an injudicious mother, he decided to seek for himself his fortune or his fate.

Commencing his new career by a rash encounter on a Mississippi river steamboat, in which he wounded (mortally, as was supposed) a fellow-passenger, he was compelled to take a harried departure for Arkansas. Alone, without a friend and without a dollar, a fugitive from justice, perhaps a murderer, a houseless wanderer in a wild, unsettled region! Fine prospects for a young lad of fifteen, and rather a peculiar "start in the world" for a hero!

Nevertheless he entered upon the task of supporting existence with no misgivings as to the future, yet without any fixedness of purpose or ambition, a fault which has lost to the world many a noble spirit, who would otherwise have left behind him an honoured name. A man seldom reaches the "mountain tops of fame" who has not placed his foot upon the ladder in early life. The eager aspirations of youth excite to the effort, while the cool judgment of manhood directs the purpose. As the hot sun of summer calls the fruit into existence, so the less heated rays of autumn mellow it into ripeness and perfection of beauty.

It would be a long story to follow his earlier career. Its many vicissitudes taught him self-reliance, and its many escapes from danger gave him a recklessness which, in after years, was exhibited to a remarkable degree in the Texas war of independence.

He had joined the first expedition into this State, where he found himself among men of tastes and dispositions similar to his own. He was actively engaged in all those battles which gave the world so strong an impression of Anglo-Saxon endurance. Fighting simply for the love of it, he cared less for the result than for the pleasurable excitement it produced. After the annexation of Texas to the United States his "occupation" was "gone," and he became an aimless wanderer once more, until at last he found himself, after many weary days' travel, on the banks of the Rio Grande.

It was at the twilight hour that he arrived there, and throwing himself on the ground at the foot of an ebony tree, he soon fell asleep, and dreamed of his home and early years, of his mother's admonitions, and his desertion of her—of the struggles he had gone through since, and the temptations he had encountered and yielded to. The sun was high in the heavens before his sleep was disturbed, but he awoke a changed man. Out of these dreams had come a determination to retrieve the past. How well he has kept his determination is shown by the flourishing settlement that now marks what was then a barren spot.

The ebony tree has been inclosed and surrounded by a seat of white plaster. It stands conspicuously at the entrance of the town, and is remarkable in this barren land for its height and beauty. It is carefully watered and cherished with feelings of sentiment for the dreams inspired under its protecting branches. It forms the favourite evening resort for the principal men of the place, who meet here to discuss their own affairs, those of their neighbours, and the nation at large, quite in the style of Goldsmith's

Hawthorn bush, with seats beneath the shade.

Clay Davis was a true specimen of the Texan, tall and athletic, yet his delicately cut features, carefully trimmed moustache, and *air distingué*, bespoke rather the modern carpet knight than the hero and pioneer of the wilderness. Association with the Mexicans had given him a peculiar style of manner, a mixture of Western frankness and the stateliness of the Spaniard; a low-toned voice, and a deference mixed with assurance.

There were many rumours afloat of his gallant bravery, and one that reminded me of David and Goliath, in which he had slain a famous Camanche chieftain in single combat, ridding the frontier of one of its direst scourges.

We do not have to go beyond our native land for material for the wildest romance. To a mind like Cooper's, Texas opens a new field, full of intense and varied interest for the novel writer.

Mr. Davis always greeted us with a welcome when we made our appearance in the ranche, and frequently sent presents of venison, game, or melons to the garrison.

He once sent me a white tea rose, the only one that had ever been seen in this part of the world, accompanied by a poetical epistle in prose, which I would copy for its intrinsic beauty, were it not too personal. It was a fine specimen of the peculiar and uncultivated natural eloquence of the West, where exalted sentiment, and what might seem to us overstrained poetry of expression, is quite natural.

These Western people have not yet been brought under the influence of the modern school of light literature originated by certain sarcastic and popular authors, who, with their thousand imitators, draw scenes from debauched life in populous cities, which turn all that is great and soul-stirring to ridicule, regarding satire on noble, elevated, and philanthropic subjects, as an evidence of high intellectual powers. These writers have done more towards destroying the poetry of life, than to elevate and improve the mind, differing widely from the quaint humour and heroic picturing of Sir Walter Scott, which cause alternately a smile and glow of enthusiasm.

Rio Grande City was first settled in 1848, and is now a prosperous village, containing about one thousand inhabitants, consisting of Americans, Mexicans, and a few Spaniards.

The buildings consist of Mexican *hackals*, the brick stores of the Americans, and the store-houses and dwelling of Mr. Davis, which front a *plaza*, where the market is daily held in the open air. The lazy Mexicans lie around in the sun, with large open baskets spread out before them, containing the most untempting merchandise, of scanty vegetables, goat's flesh, and beef, cut in strips and dried in the sun. This they sell by the yard; so that a person, in going to market, is afforded a convenient way of measuring accurately the appetite of those he has to provide for! The cakes and confectionery—made of flour, lard, and molasses—are disagreeable even to look at. Their taste it is impossible to imagine.

The *fandango* courtyard here, as in all towns where Mexican habits at all prevail, is one of the chief attractions, and forms one of its principal features; a square inclosure, with three sides benches, and one side booths, where dancing, drinking, and gambling are kept up the greater part of the night.

On the outskirts of the town the people are annually fencing in new cornfields, so that in spite of the barrenness of the land, the place looks quite thriving, having somewhat that aspect of fresh invigorating progress so generally found among our young and vigorous people, who, like poor *Joe Allalone*, are always *moving on, moving on*.

A billiard room, an eating saloon, a bakery, and even a *pharmacie*, with a most pretentious soda water fountain, are found here. All these attractions and comparative luxuries render it a place of great importance in this part of Texas.

This was a great rendezvous for filibusters, among whom could be found more true souled honesty and genuine generosity than many would be led to suppose.

Many a dare-devil Texan would scorn the paltry meanness, and fire at the acts of fraud perpetrated by friend on friend which are of not unfrequent occurrence in our civilized metropolis.

In the Texan are combined the raciness of the Kentuckian, the Creole impetuosity of Louisiana, with the reckless heart-in-hand spirit of the South-West. They follow different callings, from the scout to the office-holder under the Government, but there exist no false distinctions among them. A man stands simply on his own merits. The word *blasé*, or the idea conveyed by it, is unknown. Fresh as nature around them, their hearts beat true to the call of friendship, and respect for women seems an innate principle, while daring and bravery are no second nature, but nature itself.

The chances of life are so continually periled that it creates a recklessness unknown to us purchasers of life-preservers, who repose in the security of a private watch!

Our rides, on account of the climate, always took place towards evening. The twilight here is very short, day at its decline merging suddenly into darkness. The horses always took the same direction, the road that lay between the garrison and the ranch. It was a beaten cattle-track, cut through the *chaparral*, forming part of what had once been a race-ground used by the officers during the late war, when stationed opposite here at Camargo.

In these rides we frequently met a peaceable peasant driving home his flock of goats for their evening milking, or a band of huntsmen wrapped in gay blankets, bright ribbons streaming from their *sombreros*, returning from the day's chase with the game hung over their horses' backs.

We were obliged to ride slowly on account of the heavy, deep sand, and thickly growing briers and cacti which ran all over the ground. Walking was impossible, even if the scorpions, tarantulas, and venomous snakes lurking in the scanty vegetation, had been more rare.

There never was a country more unfitted by nature to be the home of civilized man, than this region of the lower Rio Grande in Texas. It seems to hate civilization. Everything looks discouragingly on the settler, refusing to smile on his most earnest efforts, pointing with a grim and solemn aspect to those flowery plains of the North where encouragement and plenty await him. It seems only to be intended as a home for desperate men, escaped refugees from the law; men who live in the saddle, and on the prairie seek their subsistence; such as give to Texas any bad reputation its population may have.

In this wild region deeds are sometimes enacted which make the blood run cold to read of; yet we should bear in mind the vast extent of the country, and not judge of the character of the State by the isolated acts of a roving population.

The Americans on the Rio Grande may be considered as the most daring, adventurous set of men in the world. Actuated solely by the reckless spirit of adventure and restless love fur the new and exciting, many of their lives present scenes of peril which none could encounter unless possessed of iron nerve, and which have left upon their souls the impress of a new nature.

The history of each differs from the other, yet through the character of all there runs a tinge of romance and chivalry which cannot fail to excite our admiration, although we might wish to see these strong energies directed to a better purpose.

They are essentially a peculiar race, with marked individualities belonging to them alone. Their innate nobility and high-toned sense of honour resemble more the days of Ivanhoe and Richard Coeur-de-Lion, than our more modern acceptation of the term.

The early pioneers of all our Western States were restless spirits from the colonies who, as civilization advanced, and the first settlements became thickly populated, possessing many of the restraints and few of the advantages of European cities, pushed onward into the wilderness to find, like Robin Hood and his "merrie men," a home in the forest glade, their sole companionship nature in her varied forms of beauty. Civilization, as it has followed them, has urged them, like the red men, westward. Familiar and hourly intercourse with nature has given them a tone of mind differing widely from the men of the East, who would amaze them by their "business tact" as much as they in their turn astonish these sons of trade by their hardy enduring lives of self-exposure and privation.

Since we left Texas, there has been a great overflow in the Rio Grande, and everything green has flourished. The crops have been very luxuriant. They however have been compelled to pay for this a high price, as the fever and ague has become very prevalent in consequence, "the shakes" (as they call this malady all over the newly settled portions of the West) preventing in a measure the enjoyment of this unwonted luxuriance and plenty.

While we were there the climate was very salubrious, in fact famously so; the winter days were as soft, and warm, and balmy as at the Havana. The summer-heat indeed would have been almost unbearable, were it not for the cool refreshing night breezes.

In the rainy season the river is apt to overflow its banks, and leave numerous little lakes and large pools wherever there is a depression of the ground. The soil prevents rapid absorption, and causes these to remain for weeks. In them the Mexican women can be seen at any hour of the day washing clothes, while their little naked children are splashing in the water in great glee, or lying asleep on the bare ground, under a shady bush, like so many little animals.

On ordinary occasions the river is used for lavatory purposes, and women washing their clothes on the banks, while others spread them on the brush-wood to dry, form a very pretty scene.

Towards evening it is full of bathers, men, women, and children. They swim with peculiar agility, more like water-fowl in their fearless divings, than human beings.

By driving about the country among the peasantry, at whose huts we always stopped to inquire if they had anything to sell, we became very well known among them. I finally commenced looking upon them as a new circle of friends and acquaintances.

They are an amiable, smiling, innocent race of people, utterly unconscious of the higher emotions of civilization save the feeling of sympathy in misfortune, which pervades all classes of Mexicans.

So universal is this sentiment that the bitterest enemy, in the hour of trouble, will receive care and attention. The well known devotion of the Mexican women to the sick and wounded of our army during the war, finds no parallel in history; and their love, whether for friend or lover, when once kindled, is flame in all but its short-livedness.

This lovely trait of sympathy is evident in the commonest intercourse. Their overflowing kindness of purpose, that shows itself in every trifle, has left on my memory an indelible impression of kindness towards this innocent, warm-hearted race. Yet, mild and inoffensive as they usually are, they have enough Spanish blood left in their veins to be occasionally roused to deeds of desperation and bloodshed.

The white complexion of an American and blue eyes are their *beau*-ideal of beauty, in contrast to their own dark skins and black eyes; but a negro they regard as the climax of loveliness! The more ebon his complexion, the woollier his locks, the more claim he has on their admiration!

On the Lower Rio Grande there are no slaveholders; the close neighbourhood of Mexico renders escape so easy that no slaves are ever brought here. Our coloured dependent, the only specimen of his race in these parts, was very much petted by the Mexican peasant women (who literally *adore* the sons of Africa)! The effects of this appreciation were soon visible! as I was relieved from the somewhat arduous duty of directing frequent billets (they *could not* be called *billets-doux*, as they were perfumed with a professional odour of pepper!) to a certain "Miss Georgianna, care of Julius Johnston, White-washer, Myrtle Alley, Brooklyn"! who was thus unfeelingly abandoned for the sake of a certain little sallow, black-eyed Ninetta Garcia.

I spoke to him one day with regard to his unfaithfulness as a correspondent. "I guess how's she disremembers me, I ben gone so long"! replied this coloured "man of the world." Ninetta, in the excess of her devotion, paid frequent visits to the garrison, where, with enamoured eyes, she would stand at the kitchen door and watch the object of her affection at his various and numerous employments, presuming that when they were ended he would go to the *fandango*.

Very little conversation took place between them, and that little in a language called "Mex," a kind of Spanish *patois*, differing widely from pure Castilian! This admiration for negroes somewhat disgusted me with the Mexicans, for, in spite of philanthropy, Christian charity, and liberal views, I do not believe that the coloured and white races can ever by any possibility amalgamate to an equality!

The different degrees of instinct in different races of the animal kingdom, the different degrees of beauty and utility in the different classes of the vegetable kingdom, seem a sufficient reason to believe that these same distinctions have been made in the different races of the human family.

In one of our drives we stopped at the *rancho* of an old Mexican, where we had several times before been supplied by his daughter with eggs and poultry. He had always been away at the chase, but on this occasion we found him at home; he came out to speak to "*la donna Americana*"! who his daughter said was at the door.

I noticed that he kept one of his eyes tightly closed, which gave such a droll and roguish expression to his old wrinkled face, that I could not help laughing, in which (although not knowing the cause) he heartily joined, probably from sympathy!

I put my finger on my eye, as a sign to ask him why he kept it closed so rigidly? This seemed to amuse the old fellow amazingly (he was past eighty), and in the glee of second childhood he had to sit down to laugh, saying, when he had recovered himself sufficiently to do so—"*Los Indios, señorita, los Indios*;" meaning that his eye had been shot out by a Camanche's arrow—rather a serious joke, I thought!

His name was "Chico." When quite a boy, he had been captured by the Indians, who took him up among them, picked out his eyebrows, shaved his head, and finally imbued him so thoroughly with a taste for their wild mode of life that when he was recaptured by the Mexicans, some eighteen years afterwards, he was quite loath to remain among them. But finally a Mexican wife, and several little saffron-coloured "*Bambinos*," reconciled him to his own people.

Chapter 15

Frontier Piety, Etc.

There are but few religious observances kept in this part of the world. If any Divine influence prevails it is through the instrumentality of the Roman church. On the anniversary of "All Saints' Day," we met a curious procession in the streets of Rio Grande City, carrying bright-coloured banners and flags, followed by two men bearing a long pole, on which were strung a number of wooden dolls, dressed in a most grotesque manner, wearing turbans ornamented with mangy feathers, evidently lately purloined from some unfortunate chicken's tail!

These "graven images" represented the different patron saints of Mexico. Two musicians came after them, one with a drum, and another with a squeaking fiddle, playing jigs and other lively airs, probably intended to promote religious enthusiasm! The rear was brought up by a mongrel crowd of Mexican women, babies, India-rubber or no-haired dogs, and dirty children, who were thus receiving their earliest religious impressions! In spite of its absurdity the sight was truly pitiful.

There was a current, and generally believed report, that the postmaster of Rio Grande City was a good Baptist, the only man in the settlement who owned a Bible, in consequence of which he had acquired the familiar cognomen of "Bible-back," a name that he stoutly resented! He said the Bible belonged to his wife; but he had a brother in Northern Texas who had "got religion and done well" and he thought "some" of "getting it" himself!

An Episcopal clergyman once came up the river as far as this point and preached. He had an overflowing audience, who complained that he did not give them enough "howling"—meaning a series of fearful denunciations that would serve to rouse the necessary degree of religious excitement!

It is undoubtedly the case that the Methodists are more successful than any other sect in this kind of communities. They seem to adapt themselves better to their capacities, which may be accounted for by their being a less highly educated class of men than those of the Episcopal church, and assimilating better with. It is a peculiar fact, and one worthy of notice, that since Texas has become a State the Episcopal church has looked in vain for a man to fill the bishopric, while in every portion of this country there is more need of good influence than in any of those lands where vain endeavours and enormous sums of money are annually expended on barbaric tribes who have but little intellect to cultivate, and who generally evince their gratitude for religious instruction by eating their instructors!

The pearls which are injudiciously thrown before swine to be trampled upon, in ignorance of their beauty and value, others might keenly appreciate, and carefully string and wear as an adornment. In Texas there are hundreds of intelligent human souls ripe for instruction. The heroic examples of old seem to have no power to inspire those who look upon their commission in the ranks of God's service as a worldly profession, and calculate the income it will yield! forgetting the glorious example of John, who preached in the wilderness, clothed in camel's hair, with wild honey for his food. There is a wilderness now as then to preach in, with the finest wild-cat skins, and wild honey like ambrosia!

Everyone has his destined vocation. I do not censure the old established veterans in "the army of the blest," who are needed where they are, but the young aspirants who, to use the technical expression, are waiting for "a call"—they have no need to wait—a call from heaven awaits them—let them listen! It is very easy to know and preach the right course; but, I suppose, it is not so easy to acquire the necessary strength of mind to adopt it and go to Texas for life. Human nature is so continually at war with the divine instinct, that all of us (divinity students included) have constantly to contend against those outside influences which too often turn the scale. As Spenser said two hundred years ago:

Aye me, how many perils doe enfold
The righteous man, to make him daily fall.

Although principle may at times have due weight, yet circumstances generally make the villain or the saint, which may account for the fact of Texas being comparatively deserted by the professed soldiers of the Lord.

Just at the rear of Davis's ranche, backed by a high sandy ridge, there was a long low *adobe* hut. It had a door in the centre, and two small grated windows placed near the roof. It was the jail or city prison. We had occasion once to seek a person in its vicinity; meeting there an acquaintance, "one in authority," I begged that we might go inside to see what was in there. I never made even an unreasonable request in vain in Texas, where the men are so gallant, and my wish was soon granted.

We entered the central apartment, a kind of square hall, lighted from a window in the rear, which was occupied by the jailor; two other apartments opened from it on either side, which formed the cells for the prisoners. Both were occupied. In one was a Mexican, a melancholy-looking youth, sitting on a stone bench, his head resting on his hands. Ins dishevelled lucks and sad eyes the personification of mild despair. Looking upon him as a physiognomist, I should have judged him to be a person of sweet disposition and quite inoffensive. But appearances are generally deceitful, and in this case they certainly were. He had performed a prominent part quite recently in a real tragedy.

He and a companion had been fellow-travellers from Roma, a town a few miles off. Feeling sanguinary during the night, on account of some dispute relative to the dried beef they were bringing with them to Rio Grande City to sell, he, Jael-like, had driven a butcher's knife into his friend's head, leaving it there as a token of the strength of his feelings towards him! and went on with his merchandise alone.

A party of merchants coming the same road a few hours after, discovered the body and secured the murderer, and he was here awaiting his sentence and final doom.

After hearing this story I began to discover (with the eye of a physiognomist!) a doggedly wicked look of cruelty about him, and my pity vanished with it.

In the other cell there was a person of a very different description. He was a fine intelligent-looking American, who on "a spree" had killed another man. He said that since the morning he had awaked to find himself a murderer, he had felt that he could never raise his head again. While my companions were in the opposite cell, I had a chance to hear all his woes in detail, and how dear life now appeared to him from the threshold of the grave, &c. &c.

He was a most interesting specimen of a criminal. I suggested to him a way to escape by tearing down a fallible part of the opposite wall, and as we left wished him success in his efforts, in the face of the officials, who, much to my disgust, instead of sternly trying to silence me, smiled good-naturedly.

That night Bacchus offered temptations to the jailor, to which, as many a good man has done before and since, he yielded, and my quondam friend escaped, to my great satisfaction and delight.

The graveyard at Ringgold Barracks was a sad and melancholy spot. Long dismal rows of graves of victims of cholera and massacre, with only a small numbered stick to mark each grave, the name of its occupant alone to be discovered by referring to the record book of the hospital.

These graves, in spite of all care and precaution, could not be protected from the ravages of wild beasts, principally herds of *cayote* or small wolves, who, fierce and bloody, and urged by ravenous hunger, continually prowled around the garrison at night. Their dismal howlings sounded like the moaning of the sea waves, and hilled me to sleep every night during our stay in

Texas.

These forsaken graves were principally those of soldiers from the ranks; but among them were those of two gallant officers, marked alone by a wooden cross, with the initials of their name and the date of their death. One had died homeward bound, on his route from California; the other had been drowned in the Rio Grande, seized with a vertigo while bathing.

In one corner of this desolate inclosure was the grave of a little child, only a year old, who had been buried here till the proper time of removal came. Different specimens of the cactus were planted carefully around it, where it lay by itself apart from the rest.

I often walked that way, and felt the deepest sympathy for the mother far away, who had been forced to go and leave her baby in this wretched place. As I looked at the little lonely grave, which even the wild beasts seemed to respect, for they left it unmolested, in the wilderness among the remains of murdered men, I felt the tenderest interest in the spot.

Unfitting resting-place for a little child. Yet there was another little grave beside it when I came away.

We half forget
How sunder human ties,
When round the silent place of rest
A gathered kindred lies.

The place is purified with hope,
The hope that is of prayer;
And human love and heavenward thought,
And trusting faith are there.

The wild flowers spring amid the grass,
And many a stone appears,
Carved by affection's memory,
Wet with affection's tears.

The golden cord which binds us all
Is loosed, not rent in twain;
And love and hope and fear unite

*To bring the past again.
But this grave was so desolate
With no remembering stone.*

CHAPTER 16

"The Army"

Come fill your glasses, fellows, and stand up in a row!
For to sentimental drinking we're a going for to go!
May the army be augmented—may promotion be less slow,
May our country in the hour of peace be ready for the foe;
Award each state a regiment of regulars who know
Their officers were chosen chums of Benny Havens, O![1]
Old West Point Song.

One morning there was quite a stir in camp. General Harney (that prince of dragoons) hearing rumours of numerous filibuster and Indian troubles, had come down from Northern Texas, to administer "*jesse*" generally to all delinquents, and let the community at large feel that he was "about."

Even in these wild regions the dragoons rode into camp in full equipment, on prancing horses, with their carbines and sabres glistening in the early morning sunlight, apparently just ready for inspection.

A more dashing, well drilled set of men, it is the pride of their commanding officer to know, does not exist.

While at Ringgold Barracks, some Mexican officers from

---

1. "Benny Havens" was the keeper of a small drinking-house just outside the limits of the U.S. jurisdiction at West Point. This house was the scene of many glorious "sprees," whose utter abandon would be quite wonderful to citizens. Of course they were indulged in under the most dreadful penalty from head-quarters, but in proportion to the penalty was the sup- posed manliness and nerve of the proceeding. "Benny" was a supreme favourite in the corps, and his bad liquor was ambrosia to his guests.

Camargo crossed the river to pay General Harney a visit of state; they dismounted and left their horses at the door of the commanding officer's quarters, in charge of their orderlies, who had accompanied them. These latter, tempted by the offered hospitality of the soldiers' mess-room, left their charge for a while. When the distinguished guests came to depart, they found that the silver-mounted pistols, that they had left in the holsters of their saddles, had disappeared, much to the chagrin of our officers, whose sense of hospitality and honour were very much annoyed by the transaction.

The next morning the thief was discovered among the newly arrived dragoons. I saw the meeting between him and General Harney, who stood on the *piazza*. He seized the culprit by the nape of the neck, like a kitten, and administered a good shaking and moral lecture combined, the former probably by far the most effective!

He was (as may be imagined by this fact) a man of tremendous physique, and strong impetuous passions, yet tender-hearted in the extreme towards children or animals. As I heard a Texan remark, he was "one of your high flung fellers."

This same high flung or high toned spirit is the pervading trait of our army. Mean-spirited men are the rare exceptions. The cadet breathes it in with the air of his Alma Mater, and so strong is its influence, that through life it guides his course with straightforward integrity.

On another occasion General Whiting, another specimen of our brave officers, visited us on a general tour of inspection throughout Texas. He was a polished gentleman of the old school; bland, courteous, and possessed of an affability that made him extremely popular. He seemed a man who would meet the most startling emergency calmly, yet with undaunted courage.

The "stuff" that forms our army is of the noblest kind. How illiberal are the murmurs at the expenditure that provides such a bulwark of strength to guard our outposts.

Little does the casual observer at West Point know of the after existence of its graduates, and their lives of exile and privation on the frontier, passed in lonely seclusion from the world, a stranger to its luxuries, almost a stranger to the ordinary comforts of civilization.

In our populous cities, where the refinements of life are easily attained, the officers of the army are seldom met. The wild deer, and red men of the prairie, are more familiar to them than are the people of their own race. Their lives are too often yielded in some ignoble border skirmish, sacrificed ingloriously to their country, leaving a nameless grave on some distant, unfrequented spot.

The small detachments which are scattered along our vast frontier, make up in bravery what they lack in numbers; always ready, at a moment's warning, to repel the attacks of the savages, or to pursue and punish their predatory bands.

Wherever the adventurous pioneer erects his cabin, they are there to protect him in its possession. Days of weary marching, nights of sleepless watching, whether in the *sierras* of the North, the prairies of the West, or the *savannahs* of the South, their lives are always the same. Like a chain of sentinels, their insufficient garrisons are stretched from the south-east to the extreme north-west; the reveille waking loud echoes on the rock-bound shores of Oregon, while the *tattoo* softly murmurs through the orange groves of Florida.

Chapter 17

Camargo

The occasion of a great national fair which was annually held at Camargo, an ancient Mexican town on the other side of the river, directly opposite Rio Grande City, afforded an excellent occasion for visiting that place, as these fairs bring together a large number of Mexicans, with the peculiar productions of the different sections of the country. Having been duly provided with passports, embellished with the usual flourishes of the pen inseparable from all Mexican official documents, we crossed the river, wagon and all, by a rope ferry, in a rather rickety and diminutive old scow.

We were received, on landing, by some dirty, half clothed soldiers, placed there by the custom-house officials, to see that no goods were brought into the country without paying duty. As these worthies made it a matter of conscience to steal only two thirds of all that they received, they were of course very vigilant! They looked carelessly at our passports, and we went on our way unmolested.

The city lay three miles from the shore. The drive to it was delightful, through a kind of lane, lined on either side with low flowering shrubs and brushwood. Sweet-scented flowers covered the ground, and vines clambered on each bush and scrubby, stunted tree. Their fragrance on the softened air was at times almost overpowering:—

Close fondled by the impassioned wind,
Their perfume came and went upon the sense

Like faint waves on a shore.

On our way we passed many parties going to Camargo. Mexican girls, riding on a mule's back, in full holiday dress of a short, bright petticoat, falling in ample folds, a white *chemisette* and dark corsage, with the graceful *rebosa*. They had bright, expressive faces; but their complexions were generally dark and coarse, which destroyed that appearance of refinement so essential to a beauty that can inspire a cultivated taste with admiration. The men rode on mules. Frequently a woman was seated on a pillion behind them, carrying a *bambino* for the priest to christen at Camargo.

At length a turn in the road brought us in sight of the town. The round stone tower of the quaint old cathedral, surmounted by a belfry and a massive stone cross, seemed to terminate the road.

On the immediate outskirts of the town lies a burial ground, which has been there for centuries. It is surrounded by a high, ungainly-looking brick wall, with a singularly colossal massive gateway in the Alhambric style.

There are traces of great former splendour discernible everywhere in Camargo, which was formerly a place of considerable consequence but of late years has been falling into a state of dilapidation. Most of the houses are built of stone, always but one story high, with flat roofs, and the whole place is as un-American in its appearance, both as regards the architecture of its buildings and the character of its inhabitants, as it would be possible to imagine.

A quadrangular *plaza*, faced by dilapidated stone buildings, centuries old, forms a centre from which diverge a series of streets, with promiscuous houses, some of logs, or *adobes*, with thatched roofs, and some mere shelters from the sun, that a summer wind might destroy. A few of the houses still bear traces of *fresco* on their exteriors, and many of elaborate stone carving, while the doors and windows are heavily barred, like those of Havana, giving a gloomy, prison-like aspect to the city.

This precaution is taken that the whole house may be thrown

open and yet protected. It gives the inhabitants a very small share of privacy, and a stranger walking through the streets gets quite an insight into their inner life.

We went inside of the cathedral, an antiquated pile falling rapidly into decay, where the priest (an outrageous old sinner) daily mumbles a Latin mass to a superstitious, ignorant audience, who regard even his most flagrant sins with pious reverence.

There was but one long, narrow aisle, and two transepts, forming a cross, and a high altar, with low shrines on either side; one to that once erring saint, Peter, and the other inscribed to the Queen of Heaven—some wax figures, larger than life, of the Crucifixion, the Virgin, and several of the Apostles, formed one of the most fearful and unnatural groups the imagination can picture. There was one very old and very lovely picture in the church, in the rich deep colouring of the Spanish school, representing the sweet face of Mary with the child, in which—

The maid mother, by a crucifix,
In tracts of pasture, sunny warm,
Sat smiling—babe in arms.

While we were in the cathedral a Texan whom we knew, and who resided in Camargo, came in search of us, bringing an invitation from some Spanish ladies, with their compliments, and hopes that we would pass the time we were in Camargo under their roof. I was quite anxious to see a specimen of high life in Mexico, in contrast with the peasant life, of which I had seen so much, and accepted their invitation.

Following our conductor, we soon found ourselves in an old dilapidated stone porch, its many traces of former beauty fast crumbling away, vanishing among "the things that were."

The family came out with a warm welcome to meet us, and we were ushered into a large, cool, airy drawing-room, off the front door, adorned with pictures, and leading into a dining-room in the rear, which was paved with stone tiles, the back of the room opening with a large arched way into a yard and garden in the rear, where ruined fountains and stone benches showed that there had once been extensive and tasteful pleasure grounds. A cool breeze swept through the half darkened rooms, giving a very refreshing feeling of repose after our somewhat warm drive.

The eldest sister of the family, named Dolores, had lost her husband a year before from the cholera, at the same time with her father and mother, and she with her two younger sisters had been left under the care of an elder brother, in possession of the family house. She was a widow—but not one of those disconsolate and irreparably bereaved kind, who look upon the remainder of their lives as a state of probation. On the contrary, her eyes literally glowed with showers of smiles and animation, and her rich dark hair was plaited in massive braids on either side of her face, in the most coquettish manner possible. She was not five-and-twenty, and they said her husband had been "a brute!" Some old play says *all married women's husbands are brutes*! but the play is a comedy, and they sometimes exaggerate. She was beautiful, and had what the world technically calls "a favoured suitor." Who could blame her if after a year's mourning she smiled coquettishly?

Considering the serious drawback of my speaking very bad Spanish, and she speaking very bad French, our conversation was remarkably animated, continuous, and even philosophical! I quite agreed with her that the most absurd thing a young and charming widow could do, was to barter a self-created chain of roses for the iron links of Hymen.

The two younger sisters, Inanita and Antoinette and a staid elderly brother, formed the family. These former were not as decidedly handsome or as decidedly intelligent as Dolores, although rather in her style, but as they were both redolent of "bread and butter," it was hardly fair to judge prematurely of their attractions; that bouquet must have entirely vanished, before the fascinations can fully develop themselves.

When dinner was announced I was handed with no little ceremony, by Don Jesu, into the dining-room, which opened on the garden in the rear, through a stone archway. Similar arches on either side opened, on the one hand, into a long low kitchen, and on the other into the carriage-house, where stood the massive family coach, covered with brass mountings and armorial bearings, but which was seldom used, as their means could not supply the necessary horses and men. The coach, however, remained a relic of the departed glories of their line, and was preserved with almost religious care. It seems impossible to entirely eradicate the old Castilian pride of blood.

In all the better class of houses, both here and in Havana, the room for the carriage is in close vicinity to other suites of apartments. In it the family pets generally find a home. This one was full of wicker-work cages of strange and beautiful birds, orioles and mocking-birds, those "nightingales of the south." Several fearful, unnatural-looking, but highly prized ducks, roamed tamely at large, and often found their way in very uncomfortably close vicinity to the feet of an unsuspecting guest.

A tame stork with a very vicious face, tied by the leg, made me fearfully nervous that he might escape from restraint. A beautiful little paroquet, pea-green, with a crimson top-knot and very knowing eyes, kept repeating his own praises continually, in every mood and tone peculiar to that conceited and self-appreciating race of birds. A tame fawn exquisitely small and beautiful, and a glass basin of gold fish, completed this zoological list.

The Mexican women are very fond of pets, especially a race of dogs, that are jet black, without any hair. They seem to be made of black India-rubber, and are anything but beautiful, although they are cherished with the greatest fondness by their mistresses, who manufacture a peculiar kind of soft wool cushion, of various shades of bright colours, for them to lie on. The Chihuahua dogs are rare, even here in such close vicinity to Mexico, but they are in great demand, on account of their beauty. They are less than a foot long, and six or eight inches high, looking as if they might have been imported by Gulliver, on his return from the kingdom of Lilliput.

The dinner was of a most peculiar description, to a person unused to Mexican customs and habits of life. It commenced with a compound of leeks, onions, and red peppers, a kind of soup, of which the smell was sufficient for one course. A pyramid of spun sugar, flanked by two massive silver flagons of *vin ordinaire*, ornamented the centre of the table.

The rest of the table equipage was plain and American. The second course was formed of a large dish of beef and mutton stewed together, and small apples and peaches stewed whole with it. These were piled in the centre with an embankment of mashed yellow turnips surrounding it. I was getting dreadfully nervous, for fear the dinner might pass without my sense of courtesy forcing me to taste even a mouthful of the extraordinary *viands* of semi-barbaric food.

A dish of *frijoles* at length appeared, and caused a deep sigh of relief on my part. Chickens, with rice, sugar, and pepper, all boiled up together, regardless of small feathers, followed, and then came the dessert, *dulcies* of candied cactus and melons, made by the *señoritas* themselves, which were really beautiful, a bright green, covered with a coat of crystallized sugar. A *peon* or slave stood behind each chair, besides several extra ones, whose duty it was to go to the kitchen, where two women on their knees were rolling and baking *tortillas* as rapidly as they could, which the attendants took hot from the fire, on the palms of their disagreeable looking hands, and bringing them to the table, would literally *flap* them (*vide* Johnson) down on the cloths beside every one's plate.

These are used in the place of bread; they are made of ground or crushed corn, and are baked in large flat cakes the size of sea-biscuit, on a peculiar kind of broad, open oven, which article, it is a singular fact, is manufactured for the Mexican market in the city of New York. The *tortillas* seem quite tasteless and unpalatable to a person unused to them, but are very generally used by all classes of Mexicans. It is very amusing to watch the women on their knees rolling out the dough on a wooden tray, and then baking them.

After dinner and *café noir* came the cigars and *cigaritos*. Dolores offered to initiate me into the universal custom in the country of smoking, with many jokes at my being so *au fait* for a novice, such an apt scholar, &c, &c.

I had heard a great deal of the grace with which these donnas handled their *cigaritos*, but as I had seen a *lionne* or two during my few brief summers, I thought that, comparatively speaking, they had been very much overrated.

Dolores took me to her *chambre à coucher*, and showed me many of her treasures, books, pictures, and embroideries, all of which displayed refinement of taste and a higher culture than is generally found in a place where there are so few advantages of education to profit by. They had over a dozen *peons* or slaves, whose principal business seemed to be to lie around idle, without any effort at occupying themselves more than was absolutely necessary. One of them, a girl of about eighteen, had never seen an American woman before, and got into raptures over even so humble a specimen of them as myself, saying: "*Como bella! Como blanca!*" (how beautiful! how white!)

All the *peons* crowded around at her exclamations, to look at the "*Señorita blanca*" and finally the girl could restrain her feelings of intense admiration no longer, but after patting and stroking my hands, saying they had never rolled *tortillas* (a fact which I did not deny), she gave me a sudden and overpowering hug, which entirely took away my breath. Rather a familiar and disgusting evidence of admiration!

Another *peon*, a withered old crone, almost bent in two with age, sat rocking herself backwards and forwards on a stone bench in the garden. They told me she was insane, and had been so for more than fifty years, having at that far off period been crossed in love by an officer from the city of Mexico, who, it seems, like the "false young knight" of old, "had loved and then rode away."

This old and lovelorn damsel had, since her wits had taken leave of her, lived on the public, owning no one place for a home, and yet for over fifty years she had been well clothed, well fed, and sheltered, although there were no insane asylum funds or taxes—speaking well for the humanity of the inhabitants of

Camargo.

Except the many booths where ordinary American trifles and merchandise were sold, and an extra crowd of loungers in the streets, we saw no evidence of the great national fair. We found we had arrived literally "a day too late for the fair." It had been held for the past week, and the merchants and visitors were now separating for their different homes. The last of the bull-fights (to my everlasting regret) had taken place the night before. That evening there was to be a ball and fireworks, as a "wind up" to this festal season. The fireworks of Mexico are famous for their beauty; those made by Europeans and Americans cannot be compared to them. Dolores entreated us to stay at their house all night, but that being impossible, we bade them a cordial, almost an affectionate, *adieu*, with promises of a speedy reciprocation of my visit on their part.

Circumstances which closely followed, induced them to leave Camargo and take up their permanent residence in the city of Mexico, thus effectually preventing our meeting again.

Chapter 18

Filibustering

As Christmas approached, rumours of revolution on the Mexican frontier became rife; bands of filibusters were heard of in the neighbourhood, and political intrigue absorbed all other topics of interest. A scheme had been arranged for some time past between General Canales, the general-in-chief of the Mexican militia, and General Arista, the President of the Republic of Mexico, to declare the northern portions of that country (where the latter owned vast possessions) an independent State, which in the course of time they proposed to annex to the United States, and in the meanwhile to demand our support and protection, under the new title of the "Republic of Sierra Madre."

The most prominent and active leader in the cause was Caravajal, one of the shrewdest statesmen of Mexico—a man of astute intellect, and more than ordinary mental culture. The plans of these diplomatic heads were for a bloodless revolution. The troops belonging to the regular army of Mexico had all been withdrawn from the frontier, and the militia (paid vassals and confederates in the scheme) placed there, agreeing to silently and indisputably surrender all power to him. Under this new phase of government, taxes and the custom-houses were alike to be abolished, and a free trade to be established with the United States.

These plans were confided to many of the Texan lodge of Free-Masons, to which fraternity Caravajal belonged, and as their interests as merchants were a good deal involved in the issue, they joined heartily with the revolutionists.

Caravajal was by education an American, although most patriotically devoted to the land of his birth, he had acquired a superior classical education at the University of Kentucky, where he had graduated, and consequently was mentally superior to most of his countrymen, the Mexican institutions for the education of youth being of a very inferior description.

He was a small man, with a dark complexion and an eagle eye, the beauty of his excessively ugly face—like a Scotch terrier—consisting of this very ugliness combined with an expression of great intelligence. The first time that I saw him, I was on horseback, riding across the *chaparral* to the ranch, on a shopping expedition, to purchase a few of the many luxuries to be found there. When we met Caravajal, I knew him in an instant, by the stylish way in which he wore his black felt *sombrero*, by the silver-mounted pistols in his belt, and by the pure English accent of his salutation.

The Texans, impatient for the moment to arrive when the custom-houses and taxes were to be done away with, and their goods in consequence pass into Mexico free of duty, were annoyed at the slow and decidedly un-American style in which affairs were being conducted, and therefore determined to infuse a little more "patriotism" (as they called it) into the counsels of the leaders. Through them a new turn was given to affairs, and what was in the first place to have been effected by diplomacy, was now destined to terminate in a series of sanguinary engagements, with rapine, murder, and destruction in their train. These commenced directly opposite us, in the siege of Camargo by a mixed army of Americans and Mexicans, led on by Caravajal, roused to so high a pitch of enthusiasm, that men from the ranks were daily deserting the garrison of Ringgold Barracks to join them.

On the morning of the battle we were awakened at dawn by the roar of cannon and the din of musketry that told of the engagement that was going on, within less than three miles of us. The point of the highest eminence in the garrison was a balcony surrounding the flag-staff, which was placed on a high ridge of land; a flight of winding steps led to it. We hurried there to see what we could of the fight.

The cold grey dawn of December was just melting under the warm influence of early day A few stars shone dimly around the faint outline of a new moon, and the crimson and golden rays of a southern sun glowed and sparkled on the frosty air as it rose slowly in the horizon over the mountains des Lampases.

With the exception of one mountain range, the surrounding country was flat, and on every side prairie lands lay stretched as far as the eye could see, till sky and land seemed merged into an indistinct vapour. The Rio Grande wound its sluggish way amidst its barren sandy banks, more like a wide canal than a river. The buildings of Camp Ringgold lay at our feet.

A little further up the river was Rio Grande City. Flags were hoisted from the housetops, and signs of an unusual bustle and excitement prevailed. Almost directly opposite lay Camargo, the scene of the battle. A heavy, dull, vapoury cloud hung over the country in that direction, and the firing of guns, wild yells of men and neighing of horses, in mingled confusion, came wafted to us at intervals on the clear morning breeze, giving token of the struggle that was going on between the filibuster and Mexican forces.

The Mexican troops, who occupied the town, had taken the precaution to leave their barracks the moment they learned of the approach of the filibusters, and formed on the plain, outside of the city walls. They knew by experience with what skill the Americans penetrated through the houses by making holes in the walls, thus passing from house to house, covering themselves from the fire of the enemy, until they were in close rifle distance, when, each man taking a careful aim, a deadly fire would be opened upon them such as few troops (and especially Mexicans) could withstand.

It was to avoid all this that they had determined to meet the assailants outside of the town, a manoeuvre entirely unexpected by the filibusters. The battle was therefore commenced sooner than they had anticipated. At the first fire, the Mexican allies of the filibusters fled in every direction. All attempts to rally them were vain. Many in their flight plunged into the river and were drowned. The few Americans were left alone. These gathered together around their only piece of artillery, determined to die rather than yield the field.

The Mexican foe outnumbered them ten to one. This did not daunt them. The leaden storm swept through their ranks, and thinned their numbers. Still they stood their ground. The fugitives brought word to the Americans on our side of the river of the critical position of their friends; the greatest excitement prevailed. Every American not in the army, armed himself for the rescue. The regular soldiers would have gone had they dared. Even the women wanted to go. Clay Davis, who had remained aloof until now, mounted his horse and rode out to an encampment of Carese Indians. Soon he reappeared with his face painted red, followed by the whole band of Indians, yelling at the top of their lungs, brandishing their tomahawks and spears. .

Gathering hastily into boats, they were drawn swiftly across the river, and darting up the banks they disappeared in the *chaparral* towards the scene of action.

In the meanwhile the firing had ceased. It was a moment of fearful suspense, for we thought the little band had been forced to surrender, but loud cheers soon told us that the Indians had arrived, and the firing was again renewed with redoubled spirit, and

All day long the noise of battle
Rolled among the mountains.

Happily, night came and put a stop to the unequal strife.

The silence which followed the suspension of hostilities was broken in upon at sunset by the vesper chimes, which floating once more from the old cathedral towers, on the evening air, told a story of peace, contrasting strongly with the recent conflict. The bells tolled forth a solemn requiem, that fell soothingly on the ear of the dying, and over the dead that had fallen. The atmosphere was cleared from the smoke of battle, and the domes and towers of Camargo rose up clearly against the twilight sky, the fiery crimson of a peculiar sunset casting a red glow on nature. In other centuries and other climes, this sign would have been looked upon as a symbol from Mars, smiling on heroic deeds, on receiving to his realms the warriors that had been slain.

No one thought of this, and I even heard one of our party (a major over forty) remark that the sunset promised a hot day in store for us! The world gets every day more painfully matter of fact, and the imagination becomes cramped and subdued by utilitarianism! Poets, it is well known, are yearly becoming rarer, and even a poetic temperament now yearns for a court office and salary to inspire its muse! The most daring deed, and the most glowing lyre, may linger for the moment on our ears and then pass into entire forgetfulness—a mere ripple on the smooth sea of our common-place existence. *Where, now, grow the laurel and the bay tree to furnish crowns for the poet or the hero?*

The next morning developed a most peculiar and unparalleled circumstance in the annals of war. On the previous day the filibusters came to the conclusion that as their forces were diminishing, and their ammunition giving out, they would prove the maxim that *the better part of valour is discretion*, and retire to replenish their forces and firearms, to renew the attack with more fissured prospects of success. Simultaneously with the filibusters' fit of discretion, a panic struck the Mexican troops (who are innate cowards), and as one party beat a retreat in one direction, the other party fled in an opposite one, leaving the late scene of contest in sole possession of the priests, the women and children, the infirm and the dying. These began making immediate preparations to cross (with their possessions) to the American side of the river, where they knew their lives and properties would be more secure.

Our horses were ready at the door, and we rode up to Rio Grande City to hear the particulars of yesterday's engagement. The scene that met us there was unexpectedly full of novelty and raciness. The river seemed alive with groups of refugees, in row boats and flat boats, crossing the river, fleeing from the revolutionary ravages. Children of every age, peasant women with bright petticoats and *rebosas*, aged crones with whitened locks and bent forms, tottering old men with long silvered beards, patriarchs, cripples, and *bambinos*, all that was pitiful and helpless in human nature, seemed to be wafted across, and landed on the shores, as if there were safety and protection in the very sand banks on which they landed, because they bore the (to them) sacred name of one of the United States, the home of "the proud Americans" as they admiringly call us.

Nowhere are we more respected, even venerated, as a nation than by these simple and ignorant peasantry of our border. All the vitality that they know is due to our influence, which comes to their stagnant land as refreshingly as rain to a drooping parterre, and causes civilization to flow through these regions, like its river Rio Bravo del Norte, bringing with it the only blessing this barren country has ever known.

The American elements that have spread here have given a new impulse, where but a short time ago all was torpid and lifeless. On the *plaza* were gathered clusters of filibusters, among them many who have since become doubly notorious for their daring and bravery under General Walker, at Nicaragua. Rumours of Caravajal's near neighbourhood were whispered about, and I recognised in a little dark-eyed, curly-headed boy, a likeness to the famous border chieftain, which led me to suppose his family were there also *incog*.

Most conspicuously among these men stood Clay Davis, in a red shirt, bound with black ribbon, falling carelessly open at the neck, showing linen of the exquisite embroidery of the Mexican women, a sash and belt filled with firearms, a Kentucky "toothpick" glistening in its crimson sheath among them. A slouched black hat completed his graceful costume, which, with the exception of a little extra touch of dandyism, closely resembled that of all the filibusters. I never could quite bring myself to the belief indulged in by many worthy people, that it is a sign of a weak mind to eschew clumsy boots and wear spotless linen!

Around Mr. Davis were gathered the Indians whom he had led so gallantly to the rescue. They belonged to a tribe once brave and famous, now dwindled down to about two hundred warriors; they were on excellent terms with the Mexicans and Americans, from whom they had learned, by occasional intercourse, some of the rudiments of civilization. Hearing of the warfare that was in prospect, they had come down from their northern retreats to offer their services in the cause of the revolutionists, of course expecting some remuneration in the way of plunder, or otherwise, as I do not think well enough of human nature to imagine that disinterested good fellowship alone could inspire a band of two hundred men simultaneously!

They were dressed in the skins of wild animals, bound around their loins, their hair parted in the centre of the head, and braided down their backs in the style of the Misses Kenwigs. They were armed with bows and arrows, and rifles (supplied of course by the Americans), of which they had learned the use with great aptness. Every man had an arrow peculiar to himself, so that after the fight was over each one might ascertain with certainty who could claim the scalps of the slain.

Several squaws accompanied them, dressed in wolf-skins, with bead work belts and moccasins. Their countenances were unattractive and inexpressive; evidently they were not troubled by any useless sensibility; they looked more like men than women. They had with them several little copper-coloured *papooses* strapped down most unmercifully to a shingle, on whom they seemed to scorn to lavish those little foolish endearments so natural and spontaneous to the maternal heart. They rather treated them like little faggots that some stern necessity forced them not to entirely abandon. A tiger cat with its cub that I once saw might have put their stolidity to shame! The main portion of these lovely females were encamped with their children some few miles distant—it was only a chosen few who had been brought down to the ranch.

While we stood looking on at this motley group, and conversing with the filibuster officers, a new boat arrived from the opposite shore, and disgorged its promiscuous crew of peasantry and soldiers: among them a man landed, and came to report himself to an officer who was talking to me, so that I had the full benefit of his words. His name was Sam Stevens, evidently a private, and a person of some consequence with his confederates, who gathered around and hailed his advent among them with a loud shout of welcome, one of them exclaiming, "Here's a feller that's real weather-proof, he was shot in the eye by a cannon ball, and it couldn't hurt him!"

To this, Sam modestly remarked, with a broad deprecating grin, "Well, it was something of a jar!" which speech was received with a perfect howl of delight by his appreciative audience. Thus encouraged (first touching his hat gallantly towards me), he gave us a spirited account of yesterday's engagement, telling how Major D. had "spit fire on them greasers" with his rifle, and led on the forlorn hope, with a tremendous amount of "pluck." From this his discourse flowed off into a wild rhapsody on "the great cause," making abundant use of the words sovereign people, freedom, liberty, and other expressions peculiarly American in style, all of which was received by his audience with rounds of hearty applause. I could have remained for hours, listening and observing, with intense interest, the proceedings of these varied characters, but being with "the officer of the day," who had to return at the stroke of the hour to make a tour of inspection of the garrison, we turned our horses' heads reluctantly homewards.

On the following evening, as we were taking our accustomed ride towards Rio Grande City, we met a group of Mexicans and Texans bearing the corpse of a man across the *chaparral* towards the garrison burying-ground. He had fallen in the engagement, yesterday, mortally wounded, and had died that morning on the American side of the river. We paused as they passed, and one of them handed us some papers that had been found on the body, which was wrapped in a Mexican *poncho*, and laid on a rough bier. He was young, in the first flush of manhood; his finely-cut features showed refinement as well as beauty. I knew instinctively that there were those living whose blood would have been checked in its course, could they have seen him as

In the twilight cold and grey,
Lifeless and beautiful he lay,

no hand of affection to smooth the tangled masses of his hair, or to show those last tributes that love alone can offer to the dead.

I kept the papers that these men gave me, and feel no scruples in giving the inferences that I drew from them, as I never found a clue to his history or even his name. They consisted of some notes of filibuster life, and his letters, one evidently from his mother, written in a delicate tremulous hand, although the signature and superscription had been carefully destroyed. It begged her "dearest boy" to come home, as she could not live long without him. The other was from his lady-love, and to the same effect. I felt much more sympathy, however, for the former than for the latter, for as a general rule bereaved lady-loves are consolable—but no new affection can efface the image of a lost child from its mother's heart; no time entirely dry up her secret tears. There can never cease to be moments when through the *vista* of years her grief will seem as if of yesterday.

The United States Court was to sit in Brownsville in a few days, to try all of these men that could be captured for a breach of the neutrality laws. The people there, as well as the press, took the warmest interest and felt the deepest sympathy in the success of the revolutionists, while the Court and the United States officers (whatever their private feelings may be) were in duty bound to frown on their proceedings. Rumours that the Texas Rangers, lately disbanded from the United States service, were on their way to Rio Grande City, were very prevalent.

Their object was, to get on the wilds of the prairies further north, beyond the influence of the law, and do all in their power to aid the filibuster forces in what they regarded as a righteous cause. Our government ordered that officers should be stationed with a certain number of men and pieces of artillery all along the river to prevent American citizens from crossing to the Mexican side, and joining what it denominated the rebel forces. This however was a very difficult, almost an impracticable thing on so extensive a line; the most they could achieve was to prevent large armed bodies from crossing. Smaller parties could not be stopped, and it was very easy for these to rendezvous and organize on the other side. Parties of troops were sent out from Ringgold Barracks to disperse any armed bodies that they might encounter, and in this way allay the excitement on our side of the river at least.

One of these parties encountered General Canales, the greatest guerrilla chieftain of Mexico during the late war with the United States. These guerrillas correspond to the "minute men" of the revolutionary war, who pursued their everyday vocations, unless the enemy came in their immediate vicinity, when, at a moment's warning, they took up arms and assembled for battle. Canales had been probably the most deadly enemy our army had among the hosts of their Mexican opponents.

Since Caravajal had broken faith with Arista and Canales, by telling their schemes to the Texan free-masons, they had ceased to act in concert, and when, from the Mexican shore, the latter saw a body of regular United States troops with two officers, encamped on the river's bank, he knew intuitively their errand, and raised signal flags to attract their attention. This accomplished, an American soldier was immediately despatched in a "dug-out," borrowed from a Mexican whose *rancho* lay close by, and it soon relanded with this bloody chief, who with extended arms warmly embraced the American officers, many of whose friends had fallen killed or wounded by his hand.

After this affectionate yet unpleasant embrace they drank a pledge of good fellowship, Canales drinking out of a silver flagon, which I still preserve, and which at that time formed part of the camp equipage of one of the officers of the party. He was a corpulent, greasy, and benevolent looking gentleman, saying more overwhelmingly civil things in the space of five minutes than he had ever felt in the whole course of his life, with more grace of manner than it would be supposed so stout and elderly a person could muster. The Mexicans are full of a kind of stately Sir Charles Grandison grandeur and dignity, which might be imposing to a person possessed of an impressible mind, but under other circumstances it appears forced, tiresome, and even absurd.

Knowing some of the outlaws quite intimately, I accepted an offer from one of them to send a message to the party who were in search of filibusters. Cavarajal's courier came and received my commission, and after riding express to deliver it, rode on to inform him of the whereabouts of the party of regulars who were on his track! My dreadful infringement of etiquette was however gallantly winked at, and afforded a great topic of amusement to all parties. Rigidly observed orders would have produced a civil war, instead of attaining the desired object of suppressing revolution, and there was no little good feeling existing in many instances between the parties of the pursuer and the pursued.

CHAPTER 19

Los Indios

In a wild, picturesque spot near the banks of the river, some miles above the garrison, the Carese Indians had pitched their camp. Here they had left their squaws and *papooses*, when they joined the filibusters in their attack on Camargo.

A company of mounted infantry was going that way, where it was reported there was some grass growing. They were going out in search of it, to give their horses the unwonted luxury of a few hours' grazing. We took advantage of this escort to pay a visit to the Indian encampment.

We started very early, while still—

The maiden glory of the morning star
Shone in the steadfast blue.

Before the sun had begun to dry up the night's dews, our horses were at the door. It was a delicious southern winter's day—

A dewy morn,
With breath all incense, and with cheek all bloom,
Laughing the clouds away, with playful scorn,
And living as if earth contained no tomb,
And glowing into day.

A body of armed men rode in advance of us, and the rest followed in our rear. So we rode across the unbeaten prairies, with nothing but occasional sandy ridges to obstruct our path. Vast level plains lay on every side of us, with their scanty covering of weeds and wild flowers, the clear, bright blue sky overhead, cloudless except a few white vapoury masses, while the soft perfumed air of a tropical December stole over the senses like the faint odour of violets.

The clashing of the sabres, and the steady, monotonous tramp of two hundred horses, did not destroy the influence of the scene. Our escort moved at a gentle pace, a trot or canter being impracticable for any distance, as we were pioneering our own road, and a strong chance of unknown impediments lay before us. A walk, too, seemed more in harmony with the atmosphere and its influence.

The Indian encampment, with its "cone-like cabins," at length came in view, and we drew up our horses before it. A young chieftain, about ten years old, came out to look at us. He had a bright copper-coloured complexion, and long, straight, black hair. In his hand he held a bow and arrow, quite in the style of "one little Indian boy!"

"*Picayune! picayune!*" he showed his knowledge of the English by calling out—the only word he knew, and he made very free use of it. After receiving one of these coins as an encouragement to pursue his studies as a linguist, he disappeared; but soon returned, with his sister, a young squaw, the difference of whose appearance from the other women of the tribe was very striking. She was the most beautiful specimen of humanity that I ever saw, dressed in a wolf-skin blouse, embroidered with beads, her long hair, plaited in a hundred braids, falling around her in ebon masses. Her face was cut as if with the chisel of a Phidias, the nostril, mouth, and chin a study of beauty—"beautiful disdain" (of which she probably was incapable!) expressed in every delicate curve.

Her large, liquid, dreamy eyes, with their heavy lashes, which seemed to require an effort to raise them from her cheek, through which shone a faint red flush that bespoke the Anglo-Saxon blood which rendered her Indian beauty so peerless. When she raised her eyes in their wonderful and dreamy loveliness, they seemed to deluge the spectator with beauty. She went into a tent and soon returned, bringing us an offering of milk and watermelons. A number of young Indians of all sizes and ages, quite "*al fresco*," surrounded us, begging for *picayunes*, which urgent demands soon caused the supply to fail, and the bank to suspend payment.

We did not dismount, as we found the report of grass to be without foundation. The sun may have scorched it up, or it may have been cut for their cattle by the Indians. Whatever the circumstances were, we could not find it, and as the afternoon was waning, we left the camp and returned homeward.

The cabins looked dirty inside, and the squaws and children *ditto*. They could not speak to us, and seemed more frightened than pleased, so that our visit was not as gratifying as I had anticipated. Our ride home I felt to be very perilous. My fears pictured a lurking Camanche in the shadow of each bush; we however reached home in ignoble safety. Reports of lurking Indians were so rife that my want of valour may be pardoned.

Some little time after this visit, one of the warriors of the Carese tribe came down to Ringgold Barracks partially on a tour of inspection, and partially, I suppose, to return the courtesies of our call. One of the sentinels on duty forbade his entrance, on the plea that he had not on a square inch of garment! The aborigine was inclined to dispute the point, when the officer of the day appeared, and insinuated, as delicately as possible, how much pleasure it would give us to receive him in a little fuller dress! He took the hint and departed, appearing a little later in the day, arrayed in the imposing costume of a voluminous white cotton sheet, looking like the sail of a schooner at half mast!

This delicate tribute to our more fastidious tastes, or (as he might have regarded them) false prejudices, obtained for him an interview, and I had an opportunity to prove that it did not require an educated taste to appreciate French *bonbons*, with which I regaled him; for this "red man of the prairies" devoured them all most remorselessly and with evident gusto. I wonder if the noble Hiawatha would have done the same! I hope not, for the sake of poetic association!

About this time the Camanches became very troublesome in the neighbourhood; several dreadful cases of murder and rapine occurred in our immediate vicinity. The commanding officer considered it his duty to send off all the officers and most of the men to try and terrify this daring foe. He remained himself at the garrison, with a small number of men, not sufficient to defend it properly, however. I felt very solitary in the nearly deserted camp, entirely alone in my little house.

At night I never dared to light a candle, for fear of giving a better aim to the arrow of some rascally savage without. My black esquire used to go off to *fandangoes* every night, and I was deprived of the companionship of my only protector, old "Jack," a black tan terrier, with the most roguish ears and most "druv in" of tails, by his wild excitement whenever he heard a drum beat. He slept in my room for two nights, but at reveille he would rouse me by a fit of barking that rendered him intolerable! I gave him in charge of one of our sergeants, who professed a very warm attachment for him, saying he "loved him better than his own child that he had left in the State of Maine," which triumph over paternal love I rewarded by giving him Jack for his "bunkie!"

Jack used to come and scratch with his yellow foot at the door to get his breakfast every morning, and ask for it with his bright brown eyes and most insinuating tail. On one occasion he almost tore a looking glass down, and had to be put out of the room. The next morning it was removed, and we found a sufficient excuse for excitement in an enormous tarantula, superintending a brood of young tarantulas who had recently come into existence. These are spiders of the size of a small crab, with a venomous sting, from which immediate death ensues.

As the sergeant, who destroyed this nest, remarked, "cannon-balls and firearms ain't anything alongside of one of them fellers!" In the daytime, when the sun shone, and the delicious atmosphere tempted me to spend the whole day on the *piazza*, seated in a hammock, reading or dreaming of what I had read,

Wandering through the quiet land of thought,
Where all was peaceful—

then I felt very brave; but with the shades of evening an absolute terror would fall on my heart. I would then go into the house, and barricade the windows—an unnecessary precaution probably, but one that it was impossible to resist. Then sitting in the dark, listening to the howling wolves, thinking at times, when one sounded louder than the rest, that it was the dreaded war-cry of the Camanches—I blush to record that, in spite of all my preconceived valour, I prepared myself to rush to a pantry, where I had determined to lock myself in. The agony of terror endured during this period was such as to destroy all claims of ever being looked upon as anything approaching a heroine.

Nearly two weeks passed thus when the scouting party returned. The Indians had fled in alarm before them, and for the time our prospects of undisturbed peacefulness were encouraging.

CHAPTER 20

Camp Life

Garrison life, in the phase that I saw it, was very pleasant. Each hour was marked by some peculiar military signal. At daybreak "reveille" sounded musically on the drowsy ear; then came the "sick call," especially agreeable to "Old Soldiers!" Then the dulcet airs of "peas upon a trencher," or "roast beef," summoned the soldier with fife and drum, to his frugal repast of "junk" and hard bread. Guard-mounting, morning and evening drill, parade, and finally tattoo, systematically divided the day, without rendering it monotonous.

Each officer took his turn in superintending the details of garrison duties. "The officer of the day" visited each sentinel, at daybreak, at sunset, and again at midnight, besides a noon-day tour of more minute inspection.

The strict discipline and subordination in which the men in the ranks are kept by their officers is truly wonderful to a civilian, used to dealing with that independent race of subalterns who are legally entitled to "give warning," if displeased by any trifling restriction!

The courts-martial, which meet every month, are very severe in the punishment of disrespect, drunkenness, or any other of the amiable weaknesses to which the rank and file are prone.

One delinquent was sentenced to wear a "barrel jacket" every day for a week. It consisted of an old flour barrel with a hole cut for his head to pass through, and a pair of holes for his arms. This was a reward for a chronic tendency to "spree," which somewhat interfered with the strict performance of his military duties.

The men were drilling constantly under the supervision of the sergeants; the officers drilled them only once a day. Cavalry drill was my especial delight. The officer and his jet black blood horse seemed one object, so perfectly did the motions of the horse and rider move in unison, either heading a frantic charge, or with his platoon prancing gracefully forward, and then with an unexpected manoeuvre turning swiftly on the imaginary foe.

The soldiers of our garrison belonged to that horse marine class "mounted infantry," so that drilling them into dragoons was by no means an easy or pleasant task. Without a knowledge of even the first principles of riding, they sat on their horses like a parcel of clothes-pins, and it was not an unusual thing to see a dozen dismounted at once, and lie sprawling on the ground; they were instantly up, however, and in their saddles to try it once more. In spite of their mishaps, they seemed to enjoy it very much, and after a few months' perseverance became quite a presentable cavalry company.

"Swearing like a trooper" is a very graphic expression, for if the most sanctified divine, knowing the beauties of a well performed cavalry manoeuvre, were called upon to perform the task of drilling raw men to the duty, he would have committed this ungentlemanly sin almost spontaneously.

This course of mounting the foot regiments was adopted to increase our resources in sending out scouting parties after the Indians, who at certain seasons were very troublesome and dangerous. These scouting parties, when equipped to start on their perilous but exciting adventures, presented a very spirited picture. The officer was generally dressed in a dragoon fatigue jacket, with gold shoulder straps and buttons, a broad brimmed slouched *sombrero*, and a pair of boots with sheaths of leather to the waist, to protect him from the underbrush through which he was forced to ride a great part of the way. A belt full of pistols, a sword buckled to the side, and a six-shooting rifle, composed his supply of firearms. A powder-flask hanging from the belt, and a canteen of water, with saddle-bags of limited size and capacity, held all the stores that he could take with him for a week.

The shirts worn on these occasions would produce a nervous shock on the sensitive nerves of a certain class of *petits maîtres*, whose ideas are confined to the line linen and delicate cambric of a *chemisière à la mode*. They are composed of a dark blue check material, warranted to last a week, and are in great demand where laundresses are scarce. They are termed "Old Hickories," cost exactly fifteen cents, and are generally used by hunting and scouting parties in this part of the world.

The men were equipped something like their officers, and a few loaded mules with a limited store of provisions accompanied the party. The deer and other game which they might shoot on the way were cooked on a stick before the campfire when they halted for the night to prepare their primitive meals and take a few hours' necessary rest. Sometimes they rode by moonlight, and chose the heat of the day for rest and sleep. The first thought of the men on halting is for their officer, whose simple arrangements for repose are soon made; his saddle furnishes a pillow, his overcoat and blanket a bed.

Too frequently a fatal termination gives a painful and never-forgotten interest to this peculiar kind of military duty, as was the case with a scouting party that went out from Laredo (the next military station on the Rio Grande above Ringgold Barracks).

It consisted of two officers, about fifty men, and the Indian guide, the former both boys in years. They started out with the usual equipments, and on the second day after following an Indian trail, came to a point where it suddenly disappeared, and no traces of it could be discovered.

The guide, with all his practised keenness, was at a loss which direction to take, and it was finally decided that they should separate and go in different directions. They drew lots for the guide, who remained with Lieutenant V., while Lieutenant H. took an opposite direction. They bade each other a gay and friendly farewell, with expectations of meeting again in another week at the garrison at Laredo, each boasting of the scalps and trophies they would show on their return.

Harry Love, the guide, who remained with the former party, was a character whom it is worth a slight digression to describe. He was originally from Vermont, and by his frankness and fearlessness in a measure redeemed his native State in my somewhat prejudiced eyes. His physique was that of a real "Green Mountain Boy," six feet three, and stalwart and robust in proportion, as bold and intrepid as a lion, with a voice of thunder, and a mild blue eye, which softened the otherwise fierce aspect of his rough, sunburnt face, which was half concealed by a flowing beard and heavy moustache.

When a mere boy, he became disgusted with the restraints of home, especially the petty tyranny of a stepmother, and by a midnight flight sundered for ever these galling domestic ties.

At a seaboard town, he sought and obtained a situation as cabin-boy on a vessel bound for the West Indies. When fairly out at sea, he discovered that he formed part of a buccaneer crew, whose exploits on the Spanish Main he would only allude to vaguely in after years. Over all attempts to trace his career through the vicissitudes incident upon this piratical life he studiously threw the veil of taciturnity.

At the opening of the war with Mexico, he found himself occupying the uninteresting yet lucrative position of a stevedore at Mobile in Alabama.

The news of the critical position of General Taylor, at Fort Brown, which alarmed for a moment the whole country, created along the southern seaboard the wildest excitement. Volunteers were not wanting, and prominent among them was Harry Love. The morning after the receipt of the news, he with a hundred others set sail for the Rio Grande, to the rescue of their brave countrymen. But the old hero had fought his way through Mexican bayonets before they arrived, and Harry returned to Mobile, to fulfil a long cherished wish of his heart. As has been before remarked, "alas for human constancy!" he found that the fair object of his love had proved false during his absence, and bestowed herself on a less patriotic admirer!

Harry, in a fit of misanthropic disgust, returned to the army, and throughout the war performed the most reckless feats of bravery. He never became entirely cured of his disappointment, which seemed to have taken a hold on his heart that neither time nor the instigations of common sense could entirely eradicate. Many a bright moonlight night, on a scout, he would lie on the grass, and discuss the charms of this delusive syren.

It might have seemed weakness had he not been such a brave, manly fellow, with a mind full of native talent, deeply imbued with a noble sense of honour, learned from no other code but the instincts of his own uneducated and generous nature.

Harry became quite an adept in Indian scouting while in Texas, and frequently accompanied parties of government troops. On these expeditions he seemed to know the trail almost intuitively. A crushed blade of grass, or some other slight signal, led him on their track for miles, until some unmistakable token of their recent presence proved that his conjectures had not been without good foundations.

On the occasion of the scout to which I now allude, the trail had been lost for several days, and it seemed almost impossible to find any trace of it. The men had shown symptoms of insubordination for some weeks before starting from camp, and a few hours after the officers had divided forces, it was discovered that they were commencing to exhibit signs of intoxication. Their canteens were examined, and found to contain whiskey instead of water, which had been surreptitiously introduced after inspection previous to starting.

Summary measures had to be immediately taken. There was no time to pause in the midst of a lonely prairie, with the Camanche foe lurking near, and only a band of half intoxicated men to oppose them. They did not dare to disobey the order to empty their canteens, although no promptness was shown, and it was done with muttered curses and murmurs of disapproval. One man, more bold and intoxicated than the rest, refused, and showed such flagrant symptoms of disrespect and disobedience, that very prompt measures were called for. So he was seized by order of the officer by his sullen and unwilling companions and tied with a rope to his horse, who dragged him so for nearly a mile. This sobered the rest almost instantly, and they rode forward, knowing they had no alternative but strict observance of their duties.

The rope finally broke, and the man was soon lost to the view of his companions. He eventually recovered from the effect of his whiskey and bruises, and found his way back on foot, telling some of his messmates, with great gusto, what a sight it was to see his lieutenant, when he got his pluck up! This event, instead of producing dislike on the soldiers' part, seemed to add to their respect. The uneducated mind unconsciously and innately yields to mental sway, where decision and firmness combine to force their will, and "Private Jackson" after this was always a model specimen of military discipline. No other course but sacrificing the chances of life in one of them could have been pursued under the circumstances. There was no alternative for the preservation of the rest; prompt and decided measures were absolutely requisite.

The morning after these occurrences, the party came in sight of the encampment of the Indians, at a distance of several miles. With a wild shout, the men put spurs to their horses, and dashed over the prairie, with the speed of the wind. As they neared the camp their excitement increased, for the Indians, so suddenly surprised, abandoning their wigwams, horses, and everything, scattered in all directions, seeking safety in the densely tangled *chaparral*. The soldiers followed them into the thicket, tearing their flesh and their garments at every step; horses and riders were pierced and bleeding from the thorns, which the Indians saved themselves from by crawling on the ground like snakes.

It was impossible to trace or follow them, as the horses, maddened with pain, refused to further breast the thorns. Some trophies were secured from the camp, consisting of robes, headdresses, *ponchos*, &c, and the pursuit continued by skirting the *chaparral*.

On the following day the guide struck the trail of the retreating Indians, and, as it was very fresh, the party had strong hopes of soon overtaking them on the open prairie, where they could make up for the disappointment of the day before. About noon some figures in the far distance revived the excitement of the men, when, on nearing the expected foe, they discovered that it was Lieutenant H.'s party.

But what a sight met their view! The ground was strewn with dying men, and Lieutenant H., pierced with five arrows, was lying under the shelter of a low bush, in the last agonies of death. The story was soon told. The Indians who had left their encampment pursued by the U. S. soldiers, had met with a mounted party of their tribe whom they had joined, and thinking only of the party in pursuit had neglected the usual precautions, and came suddenly upon the party of Lieutenant H. The fight was brief but desperate.

In the midst of it, Lieutenant H. pointed his revolver at one of them, who immediately commenced to cry and shed tears copiously, thus betraying her to be a squaw, which from her dress and weather-beaten old face he would never have imagined. His innate sense of gallantry revolted at fighting even with a woman warrior, and he lowered his pistol. She seized on this advantage, suddenly veered her horse (which she rode astride) to his rear, and treacherously pierced him through with a poisoned spear. They said that he fell without a struggle. His infuriated soldiers, led on by the sergeant, who immediately took command, paid them in bloodshed for the loss they had sustained by killing eight of their party, the old heathen matron among them crying and screaming to the last over her mortal wounds! This is but one of the tragic deeds which History does not record and Fame does not trumpet, that are annually occurring on our frontier.

CHAPTER 21

Texas—Past, Present, and Future

Even now we hear with inward strife
A motion toiling in the gloom—
The Spirit of the years to come
Yearning to mix himself with Life.
A slow developed strength awaits
Completion in a painful school;
Phantoms of other forms of rule,
New Majesties of mighty States.
                                    Tennyson.

Probably no one portion of our union presents so many interesting features, or so wide a field for physical researches, as that embraced within the limits of Texas, containing as it does in widespread developments the three great leaves upon which nature has recorded the history of the material world. No less extensive is the field which her history offers to the contemplation of the political economist.

The early missions of the Spaniards, to which allusion has already been made, and which were the first attempts to settle the State, were effectually suppressed by the failure of the crops and the incursions of the savages. In the year 1714, the Spanish government becoming alarmed on hearing of the arrival in Mexico of an adventurous Canadian, who had crossed through Texas for the purpose of opening commercial relations with that country, and fearing that this portion of their possessions would fall into the hands of the French, decided that the only course to prevent it would be to renew their missions. They therefore established a chain of posts from Florida to New Mexico, which soon acquired a permanent footing. The ruins of some of these still exist, the crumbling towers, arched roofs and dilapidated walls, indicating a not unpretending style of architecture. Some of these ruins are used for government stables, others are unoccupied save by the owl and the bat.

The establishment of these missions seemed securely to fix civilization in Texas. The Spanish government was extended and acknowledged throughout the settlements, soldiers were stationed at the missions, and the work of converting and civilizing the Indians proceeded unchecked for a long period of time.

Towards the close of the eighteenth century, the Anglo-Saxon pioneers began to find their way to these little colonies. They were soon followed by others, and in 1812 their numbers having been largely augmented by the remnant of the notorious expedition organized by Aaron Burr, a short-lived and unsuccessful revolution was formed against the arbitrary government of Spain. Shortly after this, Mexico revolted against the authority of Spain, and after a short struggle established her independence. From that time to the present, the history of that country has been one continued series of revolutions and counter-revolutions; every page of her annals disfigured with the blood of men who had at one time or other possessed the full confidence of the people.

It was not in the nature of things that Texas in which the Anglo-Saxon blood now predominated, should submit to the arbitrary laws and exactions of this fickle and miserable race. The dissolution of their connexion was the natural consequence of tyranny on the one side and manly resistance on the other.

The struggle for independence was a severe one, and it was not until the best blood of the pioneers was shed that she proved her capacity for resistance. The names of "Davie Crockett" and "Bowie," whose chivalrous deeds and desperate daring have even now the semblance of fabled story, are engraved on the stones of the Alamo, which will always be regarded by the Texan as a new Thermopylae.

On the 3rd of March, 1837, the independence of Texas as a nation was acknowledged by the United States, and two years after by France and England.

But the maintenance of a separate existence among nations required greater exertions than the infant colonists possessed. Besides, they had not fought for power, but for freedom; this once attained, their thoughts reverted to the prosperous land from whence their adventurous steps had brought them. It was their birthplace, the homes of their brothers, and contained the graves of their fathers. An irresistible impulse led them to seek admission into the Union. This was accomplished in the year 1841.

Hazardous as was the experiment to us, the sequel has proved, that this political exotic, transplanted from the enervating and sickly soil of Mexico, has, under the genial influence of our institutions, grown into a vigorous and hardy plant.

Texas is a State of enormous area, being six hundred miles from east to west, and four hundred from north to south, containing nearly two hundred and fifty thousand square miles, as large as the New England and Middle States combined. It contains a population of three hundred thousand inhabitants exclusive of Indians. The greater portion of the settlers are from the older States; of the foreigners a large proportion are Germans.

The main object of emigration of course is agriculture. The most remarkable physical feature of the State is the extraordinary number and extent of the rivers, having a total length exceeding ten thousand miles, which with their thousand tributaries penetrate to almost every part, causing the soil under the hand of the husbandman to yield abundant harvests. The wild luxuriant growth of the forest trees, along these river banks, have by their overhanging branches, and by falling into the bed of the stream, forming natural rafts, prevented extensive navigation. The valleys of these rivers will in a short time yield the great bulk of the cotton and sugar of this country.

Considering her comparative infancy, Texas stands among the slave-holding states unrivalled in cultivation and production, in energy and enterprise, in intelligence and morality. Any attempt to estimate her future must fall short of reality. It is impossible to comprehend the full force of a silent, progressive, and widespread emigration. The tread of armies may be realized—they move in masses, and appeal to the senses; but millions passing individually, are unperceived, until by a united action they make themselves known and felt.

Thus it is with Texas. It is only in the light of history that the effects of its annexation can be fully comprehended, coupled as it is with the history of the Mexican war, and the discovery of gold in California. It is only in the light of history that we shall be able to read the now silent workings of a new and peculiar phase of civilization. Yet there is no doubt that were the rest of the Union to pass from existence, there would yet be left, within the limits of Texas, the elements of a magnificent empire.

Land of the future, which a faith sublime
Fills with rich increase,
Hail I though conquered time
Not yet for thee has harvested the Past,
Thy seed through far horizons now is cast,
And grander spaces open for thy hand:
Thy skies are blue, and green thy fruitful land.
Ages shall pass before thy youth shall see
Fulfilled the promise of thine infancy.
De Trobriand.

Chapter 22

The Last Tap of the Drum

Our residence on the frontier was now about to terminate. Orders had arrived from the Head Quarters of the Division, at San Antonio de Bexar, for the troops at Ringgold Barracks to proceed to the north-western portion of the State, five hundred miles into the Indian country. They were to thread their way through a hitherto unexplored region of country, and if they escaped from exposure and the savage foe, to make an encampment on some carefully selected spot, where a stream of water, and perhaps a clump of trees, would supply the necessary requirements for a new military post.

Rumours of beautiful forest glades, salmon streams, countless herds of buffalo and doer, and a fine, salubrious climate, were dwelt, upon in such pleasant anticipations, that the perils and discomforts of the march were lost sight of less food, and fewer of the bare necessities of life than we had at Ringgold Barracks, we knew would be inevitable; but "where glory leads the way" a soldier seldom hesitates, although in the more sober paths of duty he may not always be found "madly rushing on!" The prospects were, that we should live in tents for two years, before which time quarters could not be built. The soldiers were to hew the trees and build log cabins, nails and carpenters' tools being all the aid that Uncle Sam furnished towards this object.

I anticipated the trip, as an additional phase in a sort of gipsy existence, with great pleasure, as by this time I had almost succeeded in forgetting the luxuries and necessities of civilized life.

A piece of hard bread and a glass of lukewarm water (strained through a rag) could not be called a banquet, yet was not an unusual meal to me. I became quite out of the habit of having any regular dinner at one period, and made up my mind to regard it as a mere unnecessary ceremony! Our arrangements for the march, however, were abruptly broken in upon, as far as we were concerned, by the arrival of an unexpected leave of absence from the commander-in-chief, and in a few days the more civilized metropolis became the goal of our journey, instead of the wilds of New Mexico.

I left Ringgold Barracks with as much pain as pleasure, feeling that had my lot been cast there, it had not been an utterly cheerless one. The climate was delicious, the life neither tame nor monotonous. I left behind me warm hearts, and brought with me sweet memories, and new and enlarged views of life as it really is, robbed of conventionalities. The people by whom I had been surrounded, though bold, reckless, and perhaps rough in their exterior, had exhibited a standard of honour and true refinement more elevated than that generally acknowledged by the world, and divested of all false gloss.

Our sail down the Rio Grande was the repetition of the voyage up. We passed through Brownsville hurriedly during the night, and drove by moonlight to Brazos Island, resting again at the wayside hut. The night was beautiful, the full moon casting an effulgence of light that seemed almost like day, producing that exquisite effect on nature, half of beauty, and half of mystery, so unlike the glare of sunlight. I was almost too weary and sick to enjoy it, for although my Texas campaign might have been invigorating to the mind, it certainly had not been so physically.

At morning's dawn we went on board the steamer, and in a few hours set sail for New Orleans. I was deplorably sick during the voyage; in consequence of which, after arriving in New Orleans, we remained there nearly a fortnight to recruit. We were to return to New York by the inland route, and secured rooms on one of the Mississippi river steam boats as far as Louisville. It was a magnificent vessel, far too beautiful for the vulgar herd that thronged it. My state-room was quite *à la petite maîtresse*, with a toilet table trimmed with lace, and pink and gold china—I believe the state-room *par excellence* of the boat.

I spent most of the week that we were on board the *Magnolia*, on deck, enjoying the sublimity of this mighty and glorious river, musing promiscuously on—

The beautiful, the grand,
The glorious of my native land.

Visions of Father Marquette and Ferdinand de Soto often crossed my mind, as we passed over the dark waters that centuries ago were first traversed by them, and my eyes were fed on the same gorgeous scenery that at every turn in the river met their view. Sublimity, vastness, and grandeur are the chief impressions produced by this peerless and mighty flow of waters.

At times when nearing one shore, the opposite banks would seem miles away in the distance. Occasional bluffs and broad spread valleys, with towns, villages, and settlements in incredible numbers distributed along, gave food for many reflections on political economy, and philosophy generally.

The rush of commerce on these western waters seems almost a miracle, so short a time ago the skiff of the aborigines or the breath of Heaven alone disturbed their repose, while now they are hourly plied by steamers freighted with humanity, urged on by an unthought of power to emigrate to the unexplored and beautiful regions to which they are hurrying—some in quest of wealth, some of excitement, others of a new home.

Enterprise—avarice—adventure—so are our human passions ordained to fulfil the destiny of the universe! It is rather common-place to expatiate and wonder at the strength, energy, and vigour of that young giant "Sam," with his many foibles, and his many noble traits—the impetuosity of his Creole blood contending with the caution he has inherited from his Pilgrim Fathers, the stolidity of his *burgomaster* ancestors, and the poetical sublimity of his Indian progenitors; the chivalry derived from some scion of a noble house mixed with the democracy of the plodding sons of toil, and dashes of religious enthusiasm with occasional touches of patriotism.

What wonder that he should be such an anomalous character, with such an anomalous combination of antecedents!

To be sure his shoes are hobnailed! and he may be seen at noon-day in a dress-coat with brass buttons! while bathing he does not regard as the end and aim of man's fleeting existence! But he is a hard-working man, and as yet has had but little time for trifling outward adornments. His ambition is insatiable, and like a young Hercules he is manfully fighting in the vanguard of the progress of humanity. Calling upon Europe to disgorge her slaving peasantry, and to ship them over where they may be illumined by the divine light of Knowledge in his happy land! at the same time nobly standing by the principle that "Cuffy" was especially provided by heaven as an exception to prove the rule, that *all men were born free and equal*, and to hoe his rice and cotton fields!

The dense forests that for miles at a time line the banks of the Mississippi are one of its peculiar features, and seem to date back to the time when *God created all green things*. No words can describe their luxuriance and wealth of form and foliage; the rough woodman, in his clearings, has frequently left a single tree standing by itself in its bed of rich emerald sward stretching out its beautiful arms, in so voluminous a green shelter, that it seemed to ask that a homestead might be reared under its protecting shade. I used to sit for hours, fascinated with all this novelty and beauty—when *the sunset lay before us like a dream,*—when the sun first rose in the dewy freshness of early day, and when nature was bathed in the silver light of the moon's rays.

Our party of fellow travellers in the first cabin were very amusing. An actor who resembled the description of that most fascinating burglar, Paul Clifford prior to his reformation, with a romantic air and a turned down collar. A bride of forty summers (or rather winters), with her second husband, gave me most intense pleasure. She used to relate anecdotes of "her dear old first," whom she represented as "a nice old gentleman," a little touchy to be sure; but that was natural at his age. She loved to dwell on the happiness she had enjoyed when daily combing his scanty grey locks from the rear, she tied them on the top of his shiny and venerable head with a black ribbon; and she would feelingly dilate on the agony of mind she endured when performing this task of love for the last time on his inanimate clay.

A month afterwards she married her "dear Joshua," a tall, slim, cadaverous-looking person, with whom she said she was enjoying her "honeymoon number two." This vulgar institution of honeymoons was intended for this class of people, I am sure!

Joshua (she said) was not as touchy as "dear old number one" on most subjects; but he adored her, and was jealous—unhappy female! She was fat and fair as well as forty, and wore an inexhaustible amount of jet finery (tokens of her recent loss of dear old number one).

Paul Clifford had a professional eye for scenic effect, and led on by encouraging glances from this bereaved bride, he gazed at her theatrically for hours to the great agony of Joshua, who made his jealousy very evident, and vented it in private on the partner of his bosom.

If Joshua had a weakness, it was for a reckless display in dress! Frogs were his ideal of richness and elegance, and Count d'Orsay never felt more satisfied with the success of his toilet, than did this simple-minded man, when he issued from his state-room with a coat literally embossed with frogs and braiding. He said he had been married in it, and that it was called "an Italian boulevard," after a place in France!

The widow used to wear emeralds in her hair to dinner, and between them they kept up such a degree of elegance and good taste, that it almost supplied these deficiencies in the remaining brown linen passengers. Some months after this I met Joshua in Broadway, and, yielding to an irresistible impulse, stopped to ask him after his wife. With a look in which he strove to embody as much lachrymose distress of mind as possible, he said; 'I am sorry, ma'am, to say that Mrs. Joshua is dead!"

All that's bright must fade, etc. etc!

There was a Baptist clergyman on board, who was at the same time a ranting abolitionist. He went on shore at one of the landings, and finding a cluster of small, lightly-clad negroes looking on at the unloading of some goods, he addressed them in pathetic language—"Oh, miserable children! don't you feel the manacles of slavery on your limbs?"

One small, bright-looking darky, looking at another, said, "No, I don't, does you, Zip?"

To which Zip replied in the negative with a shout of negro laughter, accompanied by a series of gymnastic evolutions, from his proficiency in which he had acquired his sobriquet of Zip Coon. The philanthropist was quite nonplussed, but afterwards remarked it was fearful to see human souls so blind to their own wretchedness as to be able to dance and sing in a state of such deplorable bondage! Some Californians returning to their northern homes, and other less conspicuous passengers, completed our party.

On the deck below there a different class of people, and the scene there was at all times animated. A large party of flat-boat men, who had been to New Orleans with their lumber, were returning with us up the river, earning their passage by assisting in taking in firewood and freight at the different landings. Some were Mississippi River men, and others from the Ohio and Wabash, a great deal of party spirit was occasionally exhibited among them.

One evening at quite a late hour we stopped to take wood at a rough wharf near one of the clearings. The doors of the furnaces were opened, which threw a deep red glow on the shore; pine faggots were lighted on the bank, and the deck hands and deck passengers were formed into gangs to carry the wood on board. The Wabash River men commenced singing an exulting air with each verse ending "the gallant Wabash boys." This was emphatically groaned at by the others. At the end of it, one of the opposition set up the well-known air of "sailing down the river of the Ohio;" at this the Mississippi River men renewed their dismal groans, and finally followed a terrific row, which it is impossible for me to describe.

The whole scene was one peculiar to this river. The fiery glow cast from the furnaces on the shore lighted up these wild looking figures, as they worked at their task, and shouted their excited strains. The dense gloomy forests that backed the clearing suggested to the mind the vast unbroken depths of solitude that lay enshrined within their precincts. Where

> *The growths of jasmine turned*
> *Their humid arms, festooning tree to tree,*
> *And at the root, through lush green grasses, burned*
> *The red anemone.*

The evening star shone out in its pale dim beauty, while over all the shades of night were falling. At Natchez "under the hill" we took on board a most suspicious-looking set, soon discovered to be a gang of blacklegs of the deepest dye, who finding they were regarded with suspicion left the boat at the next landing above.

At all times of day and night we would be startled by a hard bump, and the general cry of "a snag" would resound. These fallen trees are shifted by each tide, and it is impossible to steer clear of them. Their great roots lie embedded in the bed of the river, and their trunks pointing directly down the stream have too often caused the most disastrous wrecks and loss of life. Between these and the reckless racing of the high pressure steamboats, a sail on the Mississippi becomes a rather perilous adventure.

The flat-boat men, on their way down the river, used to amuse me very much! They were a jolly set of reckless fellows, who seemed to think that after their boat is built, launched, and loaded, they have nothing to do but to enjoy to the utmost extent the trip to New Orleans. A fiddle and a banjo generally accompany them, and these combined with their vocal choruses principally of negro minstrelsy, floated over the waters in delightful harmony. They cook their food on deck, and form quite a picturesque group as they sit around the boiling pot from which each helps himself.

When they arrive at their destination the flat-boat is knocked to pieces, the planks which compose it sold with the cargo, and the crew work their way homeward, on some of the steamers.

After a week's sail we reached the junction of the Ohio and Mississippi, and in two days more the *Magnolia* deposited us at Louisville, Kentucky. From there we continued up the Ohio to Cincinnati, and returned, *via* Lake Erie. Buffalo, and Albany, to New York.

Here ended my brief campaign, and with it ended a chapter in a life's history only interesting perhaps to a few friends, whose thoughts accompanied me to the frontier. A soldier requires a buoyant disposition and a philosophical turn of mind more than most men, and if this can be arrived at, there is much that is attractive in his careless, semi-civilized existence.

In retrospect all the discomforts of that wandering life are forgotten, and so truly does "alchymist memory turn the past to gold" that I find "The past is very tender at my heart," and I can now only recall bright and glowing recollections of the days of following the drum.

Sounds that once so charmed my ear
I no longer now can hear;
They are all an empty hum,
For the drum! Oh, the drum!

ALSO FROM LEONAUR
AVAILABLE IN SOFTCOVER OR HARDCOVER WITH DUST JACKET

CAPTAIN OF THE 95th (Rifles) *by Jonathan Leach*—An officer of Wellington's Sharpshooters during the Peninsular, South of France and Waterloo Campaigns of the Napoleonic Wars.

BUGLER AND OFFICER OF THE RIFLES *by William Green & Harry Smith* With the 95th (Rifles) during the Peninsular & Waterloo Campaigns of the Napoleonic Wars

BAYONETS, BUGLES AND BONNETS *by James 'Thomas' Todd*—Experiences of hard soldiering with the 71st Foot - the Highland Light Infantry - through many battles of the Napoleonic wars including the Peninsular & Waterloo Campaigns

THE ADVENTURES OF A LIGHT DRAGOON *by George Farmer & G.R. Gleig*—A cavalryman during the Peninsular & Waterloo Campaigns, in captivity & at the siege of Bhurtpore, India

THE COMPLEAT RIFLEMAN HARRIS *by Benjamin Harris as told to & transcribed by Captain Henry Curling*—The adventures of a soldier of the 95th (Rifles) during the Peninsular Campaign of the Napoleonic Wars

WITH WELLINGTON'S LIGHT CAVALRY *by William Tomkinson*—The Experiences of an officer of the 16th Light Dragoons in the Peninsular and Waterloo campaigns of the Napoleonic Wars.

SURTEES OF THE RIFLES *by William Surtees*—A Soldier of the 95th (Rifles) in the Peninsular campaign of the Napoleonic Wars.

ENSIGN BELL IN THE PENINSULAR WAR *by George Bell*—The Experiences of a young British Soldier of the 34th Regiment 'The Cumberland Gentlemen' in the Napoleonic wars.

WITH THE LIGHT DIVISION *by John H. Cooke*—The Experiences of an Officer of the 43rd Light Infantry in the Peninsula and South of France During the Napoleonic Wars

NAPOLEON'S IMPERIAL GUARD: FROM MARENGO TO WATERLOO *by J. T. Headley*—This is the story of Napoleon's Imperial Guard from the bearskin caps of the grenadiers to the flamboyance of their mounted chasseurs, their principal characters and the men who commanded them.

BATTLES & SIEGES OF THE PENINSULAR WAR *by W. H. Fitchett*—Corunna, Busaco, Albuera, Ciudad Rodrigo, Badajos, Salamanca, San Sebastian & Others

AVAILABLE ONLINE AT **www.leonaur.com**
AND OTHER GOOD BOOK STORES

ALSO FROM LEONAUR
AVAILABLE IN SOFTCOVER OR HARDCOVER WITH DUST JACKET

WELLINGTON AND THE PYRENEES CAMPAIGN VOLUME I: FROM VITORIA TO THE BIDASSOA by *F. C. Beatson*—The final phase of the campaign in the Iberian Peninsula.

WELLINGTON AND THE INVASION OF FRANCE VOLUME II: THE BIDASSOA TO THE BATTLE OF THE NIVELLE by *F. C. Beatson*—The second of Beatson's series on the fall of Revolutionary France published by Leonaur, the reader is once again taken into the centre of Wellington's strategic and tactical genius.

WELLINGTON AND THE FALL OF FRANCE VOLUME III: THE GAVES AND THE BATTLE OF ORTHEZ by *F. C. Beatson*—This final chapter of F. C. Beatson's brilliant trilogy shows the 'captain of the age' at his most inspired and makes all three books essential additions to any Peninsular War library.

NAVAL BATTLES OF THE NAPOLEONIC WARS by *W. H. Fitchett*—Cape St. Vincent, the Nile, Cadiz, Copenhagen, Trafalgar & Others

SERGEANT GUILLEMARD: THE MAN WHO SHOT NELSON? by *Robert Guillemard*—A Soldier of the Infantry of the French Army of Napoleon on Campaign Throughout Europe

WITH THE GUARDS ACROSS THE PYRENEES by *Robert Batty*—The Experiences of a British Officer of Wellington's Army During the Battles for the Fall of Napoleonic France, 1813.

A STAFF OFFICER IN THE PENINSULA by *E. W. Buckham*—An Officer of the British Staff Corps Cavalry During the Peninsula Campaign of the Napoleonic Wars

THE LEIPZIG CAMPAIGN: 1813—NAPOLEON AND THE "BATTLE OF THE NATIONS" by *F. N. Maude*—Colonel Maude's analysis of Napoleon's campaign of 1813.

BUGEAUD: A PACK WITH A BATON by *Thomas Robert Bugeaud*—The Early Campaigns of a Soldier of Napoleon's Army Who Would Become a Marshal of France.

TWO LEONAUR ORIGINALS

SERGEANT NICOL by *Daniel Nicol*—The Experiences of a Gordon Highlander During the Napoleonic Wars in Egypt, the Peninsula and France.

WATERLOO RECOLLECTIONS by *Frederick Llewellyn*—Rare First Hand Accounts, Letters, Reports and Retellings from the Campaign of 1815.

AVAILABLE ONLINE AT **www.leonaur.com**
AND OTHER GOOD BOOK STORES

www.ingramcontent.com/pod-product-compliance
Lightning Source LLC
Chambersburg PA
CBHW021007090426
42738CB00007B/693